The Forester

The Forester

The Story of James Lymburn Shaw
Forester of Killearn, Tintern, and Gwydyr

IAN NIALL

HEINEMANN : LONDON

William Heinemann Ltd
15 Queen St, Mayfair, London W1X 8BE
LONDON   MELBOURNE   TORONTO
JOHANNESBURG   AUCKLAND

First published 1972
© Ian Niall 1972

434 451018 1

Printed in Great Britain by
Western Printing Services Ltd, Bristol

Contents

Prologue

F ew of us give much thought to the presence of trees in a
particular landscape. We are used to seeing them. They are
there, like many other topographical features, hills, crags,
or the rivers that wind across flat country. A row of pop-
lars, an elm shading the fly-troubled cattle, a pine tree on a
ridge, all of these are things we take for granted, as we take
for granted the hedges that bound the fields. Woods and
thickets had been there so long that our fathers were unable
to say they noticed any difference in them, and so they are
the background of our existence. They didn't really grow,
but have been there since time immemorial. That this
can't be so should be apparent even to a child. Trees die
and seedlings grow up through the grass, or in garden
beds, and we see these things happening. Nevertheless,
the continuity of tree life, the slow dying and the slow
growing of oaks and other broad-leaved trees, or even of
pines, which not many people seem to realise live to more
than a hundred, gives us no mark of beginning; no end
until a wood is cut down. The old wood has gone, we say.
It is a pity that the rooks won't be nesting in the elms. It is
a shame about the oak. It must have been there when
Cromwell was on the march. It sheltered the villagers. It is
no more. We transfer our affection to another wood,
another venerable giant of the forest, and walk through

sun-dappled beech lanes of the wood thinking what wonderful things trees are.

It is because I have always had a strong love of woods
and trees as individual living things that I chose to write
this life of a forester. I must admit at once that I had no
conception of the depth and breadth of forestry, or the
meaning of sylviculture as such, until I began to talk to the
man about whom I have written the book. I knew the old
woods of my childhood as well as anyone. I did a lot of my
day-dreaming in them, listening to the breeze hushing in
the branches of pines or the wind making the bare branches
of elm or beech swish like sweeping brooms. I felt en-
folded and secure in the forest. Since a child takes most
things for granted I never thought that nearly every wood
in the country is a wood by virtue of someone's intention
to create it so, to plant, to nurture and protect the trees
growing within its boundary for reasons that are often as
fascinating as the sorts of trees planted. Men grew woods,
railed or walled off land and cultivated trees to provide
shelter belts, wood for houses, ships, gates and fences, to
make hunting grounds or simply serve as an asset in the
economy of an estate in hard times.

Whatever the reason for the planting of woods and
forests, or even the cultivation of the hedgerow tree, conservation was the most important factor in achieving the
end. Without care a newly-planted wood would become
choked and die like any other kind of seedlings sown or
planted too close. Without care and knowledge of the
needs of trees there would have been nothing but scrub
woods, gnarled and stunted oaks, disease-ridden timber fit
only for the fire. Sylviculture is a comparatively modern
word. Forestry is an older one, although its meaning is not
quite the same, the one having more to do with the cultivation of trees and examination of the soils and the conditions upon which the growth of particular species of tree
depend if they are to grow into tall, healthy specimens, and
the other being perhaps more concerned with the mech-

anics of planting and extraction. At a time when words
like pollution, ecology, environmental pressures are on the
lips of the third or fourth form in the grammar school,
most of us are aware that somehow the world will face a
crisis if ever plant life is poisoned chemically or by some
atomic disaster. Not many of us look at the woods that dot
the countryside throughout Britain and think that our
lives are bound up with the healthy growth of trees, and in
turn, the crops which grow in the fields beyond the woods
depend on the trees. Here we have a chain of life, animal
and vegetable, in which we and the trees are links.

How can a factory worker concern himself about trees
when he is tied to the production line, or even a politician
think very much about a line of elms when he is so busy
thinking up clever things to say about the opposition? A
dreamer may dream of leafy glades and the cathedral
vaults of quiet woods but the practical business of the
wood's survival is the work of the forester. Like so many
other callings a forester's calls for great faith in the future,
faith to an extent that a man must plant a seedling beech
and look at a tree that is already more than a century old to
see what he is doing. Visionaries, one might say, plant
trees. They rarely live to see the result. They must take
heart from seeing what men long dead have left for them
to see. This goes back throughout the centuries and is one
of the mystical wonders of forestry.

The man about whom this book is written was in one
sense a simple, uncomplicated man. He accepted what he
had been taught—that time is not important except in the
diligent performance of a daily task. He planted more trees
than most men of his time, I am sure, deciduous trees by
the thousand, trees that clothe the hills of his native country, trees that flourish in the south of England now and
trees that cover a good part of Wales. He knew about soil
erosion and the life that lives in the shade of trees before
learned textbooks had been written on the subject. He
planted in the manner he had been taught to plant by old

estate woodmen of the Scottish forests. In the course of a lifetime he cultivated not only trees but the special philosophy of the forester.

I talked to Jim Shaw for many hours about his life's work. He told me how to grow nursery seedlings, how to plant and how to cut a tree down. Throughout our long talks I found him an unassuming, modest man. My difficulty was to convince him that what he took for granted was far from common knowledge. If he had any vanity it was not revealed to me. All he knew, he said time and again, he had inherited from his father and men like him, men who lived in the forest and thought about little else but the preservation of trees, watching them improve and put on growth year after year, studying their shape and form as a breeder might study a young horse. A forester's most satisfying work, he told me, is to plant for posterity— hardwood trees where hardwood does best. This mentality strikes me as being religious in a profound sense. Jim Shaw was a religious man for everything he did was an act of faith.

When I had gathered all the material for his life story I went back to Jim Shaw and asked him what he would have changed. He said he had always felt that we have been planting too many conifer trees, even allowing for the fact that the national policy of planting requires some sort of quick return on the investment. Conifers don't encourage undergrowth or allow much light and air into a wood. In consequence conifer woods are dead woods, silent places devoid of animal and insect life. They have the nature of a closed-up warehouse. The goods within the walls may be of economic importance but they are dull and ugly and infinitely monotonous. Amenity, said Jim Shaw, should have been rated of higher importance. The sporting and recreational possibilities and potential of state forests might have been more closely examined, and a certain revenue obtained from these if every investment must show immediate profit. Even the conifer woods of Britain are a long-maturing national asset but there is no reason why a civil service mentality should keep them closed to the public when nearly all of them have usable roads. Conservation tends, in this event, to become an excuse for locking away what is a generation's heritage and ensuring that it is never seen but lies, like a spinster's dowry, gathering interest never to be drawn upon. It would, thought Jim Shaw, be greatly to the advantage of everyone if a study of our national resources in forestry were made and state forests used as far as possible as reserves for creatures threatened with extinction. People could, for instance, watch the buzzard, pine-marten, polecat or roe deer, paddle a canoe on a forest lake or sleep in the woods overnight. All of this, of course, hedged round with regulations to protect the forest rather than to lock the people out from places that are, after all, the property of us all.

An old forester, and one who had spent a good part of his life planting trees in places coveted by hill farmers and the like, might have been much less tolerant of the public than the foregoing words reveal. Jim Shaw believed that the most important thing ahead of the tree-planters was to let the public see what has been done, to educate them on the subject of trees and forestry in general, so that they could better appreciate their inheritance.

Soon after this book was finished misfortune befell Jim Shaw, sturdy màn of the trees though he had been. He had to have a leg amputated and succumbed to the shock of this ordeal at the age of seventy-nine. Gas gangrene is a painful condition and Jim Shaw, strong though his heart was, died soon after the operation. I saw him shortly before he died, and knew that he would die. I was deeply touched by the shadow in his face, for he knew it too. He tried desperately to tell me just one more story of the happiness of his life in the forest. I could make nothing of it except that it was about muzzle-loading guns and keepers long ago, probably on the Killearn Estate. His ashes were scattered in a beech wood which lies within the Gwydyr Forest where he toiled so long and so well. His monument stood long before he died—eighty-feet-high noble firs and they will be there for another hundred years.

A Lad called Jim Crow

DOONHOLM Estate in Ayrshire is close to Doonfoot and the River Doon, barely two miles from Alloway and the birthplace of Burns. The Shaw family came there from Kilkerran which is hard by Dailly and Killochan in the same beautiful country. It was hardly a gipsy instinct that made William Shaw move from the estate of Sir Charles Fergusson to that of Lord Blackburn, exchanging the Water of Girvan for the banks and braes which so inspired the poet. The Shaws were far from itinerant by nature and habit. William Shaw was a woodman and represented the third generation of his family to follow that calling. He took service with Lord Blackburn not simply with the hope of improving himself, but to obtain better accommodation for his growing family. He had served Sir Charles as woodman and went to his Lordship in the capacity of head woodman, to be his right-hand man.

Even the red sandstone lodge standing at the entrance to the drive was to prove barely large enough for the family of five boys as they grew apace. The lodge stood on a flat bit of ground and was typical of estate dwellings reserved for special servants on the outdoor staff. Behind its four-square structure the ground rose steeply. There was a tool-shed and a place where the woodman could resharpen his razor-edged axes and his finely set saws. Although a man in authority, William Shaw took a pride in these things and loved to use the forester's implements or demonstrate his skill to those eager to learn how to use axe, saw or pruning tool. There was, in addition to a workbench, a log steady and a chopping block. Beyond these, a place for his beehives and a henhouse, with a patch of rough ground where the hens could take dustbaths in the summer sun and lay away among the ferns and bracken. It was the year 1896. The world was at peace. Nowhere was it more peaceful than the Doonholm estate. Pigeons cooed in the long green vaults of its deciduous trees. Pheasants crowed, and now and again the woodpecker laughed its insane laugh, forecasting rain and earning its nickname. These green woods, with their varying shade of oak, ash and beech leaves, were part of the great patchwork of the Ayrshire countryside, which altogether was a seemingly endless quilt of plough and pasture. Round green hills and brown plough or stubble were reflected in the water that ran from Loch Doon to the sea at Doonfoot. Here, William Shaw told himself as they moved, was a new beginning, a snug lodge in a place to inspire a poet. As soon as they were settled in he was due to report to his Lordship.

The hierarchy of estate service in Victorian times included several branches of the domestic department such as the Housekeeper and the Butler. It also included the Head Gardener, the Home Farm Bailiff, the Head Keeper, and the Head Woodman or Forester, all outdoor staff. Of these the woodman's duties were certainly the most widespread. They included such things as water-supply, drainage, repairs and maintenance, and provision of firewood and kindling. To keep the home fire burning, an entire Saturday would be spent sawing and splitting hardwood logs! Six or seven woodmen might be engaged on this task. The mansion used coal for cooking fires, but no one liked the scent of burning oak logs more than Lord Blackburn and the Doonholm fireplaces were large.

William Shaw was an industrious, supple man of thirty-six. He detested idleness as much as he disliked careless-ness. He had come to be his Lordship's forester and run things as he knew he would be expected to run them, keeping fences and gates in repair, checking bridges, sheds and every structure made of wood to see that nothing was eroded or decaying. The woods of Doonholm were rich in timber. Some of it, as it ripened and attained its highest market price, would be cut for commercial pur-poses. Some of it would be of less value than the timber the importuning contractors offered to purchase, and would serve for anything from rick props around the home farm to logs for the mansion fire. That William Shaw knew his trade Lord Blackburn never doubted. His neighbour had given him the highest references and said that he was not only well versed in all his duties, but no mean hand with a flyrod, should his Lordship need a salmon from the Doon.

After the first day or two the family found its bearings and explored their immediate world. The boys were for-bidden to go to the river, for James was barely four years old, and too adventurous by nature to be trusted far from the door. Even there he had already managed to create a degree of havoc by climbing the slope to one of the newly established beehives and blowing at its entrance to dis-courage the occupants from coming out! There had been a frantic search for the bluebag and a sting or two distorted young James's features. Unless William, who was twelve, and John, who was barely nine, could promise to look after their younger brothers, Gilbert and James, they would all have to stay within sight of the lodge, their father told them. Gilbert, the seven-year-old, was tolerated by his older brother. James, tiring of the game of blowing the bees, cooled his head under a water tap and came dripping into the kitchen, complaining that the others had left him behind. His mother had to cope with him and his baby brother, Robert.

William Shaw worked no set hours. He toiled away for as long as it took to perform any self-allotted task. This generally meant that he worked through the hours of daylight. He came home to read and to rest. When there was time in spring he planted his garden and hoed a row or two. He looked to his bees and helped his wife Jane with her problem of catching a rat that lived somewhere behind the toolshed or the henhouse, but there were rare occasions when he took time off. Sometimes he walked with his wife and children to Alloway, where a horse-bus gathered passengers for Ayr and there was more life to be seen than around the quiet paths and rides of the estate. Once a year there would be a special attraction, like the Ayrshire Agricultural Show or the West of Scotland Show. Flower shows were held in the Dam Park at Ayr, and then there were the Ayr Races. It was William Shaw's delight to take the boys to Ayr when the races were on. He wasn't a racing man. Indeed, he had no great liking for horses, even the docile sort of creature he might have harnessed to a gig to go and do estate business with the timber merchants. What drew him to Ayr was the sideshow, the noise and hurly-burly of the fair. To make it a day for the boys he would load young Gilbert and James into a perambulator and trundle them to town. At the coconut stall he would demonstrate that the co-ordination which enabled him to swing a great axe and split a matchstick wasn't confined to feats of this kind. He was a dab-hand at knocking down coconuts at three balls a penny, at winning dolls and butter-dishes or glittering spoons that always tended to tarnish when dipped in the jam for the first time. James and Gilbert loved to see their father knocking things down and eagerly gathered his prizes around them when at last the pram was turned towards Alloway and home.

A time came when Gilbert made the visit to Ayr on foot. James stayed in the pram watching Father perform his feats of marksmanship which so dismayed the stallholder. Young Gilbert, drawn by something more novel elsewhere, wandered away and was lost. After a brief but fruitless search the pram was set in motion and William Shaw and young James returned home.

'In all that crowd,' William said to his wife, 'how could we hope to find him? Greet, my boy? No, he'll know what to do. He'll look for a policeman! He's a Shaw and a Shaw doesn't get lost even in the forest! He has a tongue. The policeman will be here before very long bringing Gilbert back for his tea!'

Mrs Shaw frowned. She thought of all the potato-diggers, the tinkers and cadgers she had ever seen on the road to Ayr when there was a fair or a show, and she was anxious for 'Gilbert so long at the fair'. William Shaw's prediction proved sound however. Less than an hour later the little gate creaked and the Alloway policeman brought Gilbert to the door.

'He was lost, Mr Shaw, but you'll see that even if his face isn't very clean he wasn't greetin', no him! "Daddy just went away on home without me," he said, "and I forget the road."'

The Shaws were reunited. Gilbert sat down to his tea as though nothing had happened.

'I saw a calf with two heads,' he said, 'and a woman with a beard! I didn't have to pay. I just got pushed inside with the crowd.'

A less entertaining sight both boys barely escaped seeing shortly afterwards. Walking with their father, who was showing them the trees of the park and drawing their attention to birds, they were suddenly ordered home.

'Go back at once, boys,' said Mr Shaw, his voice hoarse. 'Don't stand about, and don't follow me! Go right on home to your mother.'

Looking over a hedge William Shaw was shocked to see the body of a man hanging from a tree in a copse through which he had been about to take his small sons. Mr Shaw had to cut the unfortunate man down. Before he did so, and while he was fumbling for his pocket-knife, he was horrified to see that perched on one of the dead man's boots was a robin. The family talked of the tragedy for days. Young Jim Shaw never forgot hearing his father tell of the happy robin standing so perkily on the hanging man's boot.

That his new head woodman was an expert salmon fisherman pleased Lord Blackburn, particularly when his cook needed a salmon for the table. William Shaw would be instructed to take time off from measuring and marking timber, to lure a fish from one of the pools. A certain sandstone quarryman provided the right kind of fly for the Doon. Armed with this, and one of his big bamboo cane fishing rods, William Shaw would set forth to get a salmon. There was nothing he enjoyed more than pitting his skill against a fish. He had hardly ever failed on the Water of Girvan and soon he was equally capable of dealing with the Doon salmon. A powerful frame—he was little short of six feet, long-legged and broad-shouldered—enabled him to cast with the best and put the fly down the lie in exactly the right way. When salmon were taking he could be relied upon not to fail Lord Blackburn's cook. After a reasonable length of time his fish would come to the gaff. Gilbert, who carried that instrument, would be summoned to hand it to his father so that the fish could be lifted on to the bank.

'There!' William would exclaim. 'Fresh from the sea and with the sea lice on him to prove it! His Lordship should be pleased with that. Just you take hold of it in the gills and carry it carefully up to the mansion, unless you think you need Wee James's help?'

A fifteen- or twenty-pound salmon is no small burden for a boy of eight to carry. Like most burdens it tends to get heavier the farther it is carried. Gilbert would set off manfully, determined to have no help from his smaller brother. William Shaw would watch him depart, smiling and running a hand over his mutton-chop whiskers. He knew what it was all about. The salmon would tire Gilbert long before he reached the back door of the big house and handed it over to the cook. But Gilbert would be able to put all the pennies in his own pocket, instead of sharing the cook's bounty with his brother!

'Your turn will come, James,' he would tell the disappointed small boy at his side. 'Your turn will come.'

James was always mollified by a pat on the head, but his day wasn't to come. By the time he was big enough to carry his father's catch they had moved to fresh woods.

It wasn't always bright and sunny at Doonholm. There were days when it was cold, days that were short and days when it rained, to say nothing of long nights when the hail penetrated the bare branches of the trees and water seeped over the sandstone doorstep. Jane Shaw had never really considered their accommodation adequate. The recess bed took two boys. Two more were crowded into a deal settle, that ornament of many an overcrowded rural dwelling in south-west Scotland in Victorian times.

'They are growing up. Every year that passes they grow bigger. Five lumps of boys! We'll never manage here. You'll just have to speak to his Lordship,' said Jane.

William Shaw spoke to his Lordship, respectfully and tactfully, as aware of his master's problems as he was of his own.

'Well, sir,' he said, when his Lordship had shaken his head. 'Something will have to be done. That's all there is about it.'

The head woodman earned only £65 a year. He was, of course, much better off than most. A woodman might earn £50 a year. He wouldn't have a lodge to live in, but an estate cottage. He wouldn't have quite the same perks, labour to help with his garden, manure from the home farm, coal as well as wood, if he wished, and running water at his door. The position carried a degree of prestige that set the head woodman apart from other employees of the estate, somewhere below the agent or factor, but above the Head Gardener, Head Keeper or Bailiff of the Home

Farm. Answerable only to his Lordship, William Shaw talked to his master with deference and respect, but expressed opinions on the management of the estate with a forthrightness that would not have been tolerated in lesser employees. When he needed a day off he mentioned his need to his master and received his assent, as when he had arranged for the family to go to the potato-growing country around Craigie on the coast, where Grannie Shaw still lived. The journey was made on the potato carts which returned empty after delivering the crop to the Glasgow and South-Western Railway at Ayr. South Ayrshire was famous for its early potatoes and a favourite ballad of the time was the 'Tattie Hoickers' sung to the tune of 'Scotland the Brave'.

Holidays by the sea or no, the Shaw family were feeling a certain domestic strain and his Lordship after much thought suggested that his nephew's estate in Stirlingshire, might offer a solution. If William Shaw was prepared to uproot himself a second time, and go north beyond the Old Kilpatrick Hills and the Campsie Fells, he might find what the family needed, a larger dwelling, even a brand-new house built for him by Colonel Blackburn.

'If we've got to go it might as well be there,' said William Shaw. 'I'll talk to my wife, your Lordship. It's a matter for her. If she's not happy I can't be happy.'

'Killearn?' said Jane. 'And what are we to have at Killearn?'

'A better house. His Lordship is arranging that with Colonel Peter. It depends on what you say.'

Jane Shaw thought for a bit and nodded. Very well. If Colonel Peter Blackburn had a better house for them or promised to have one built they would go north to Stirlingshire. It was 1899 and they were young enough to move and move again if need be. Soon afterwards their things were transported north to Killearn which lies north of the Campsie Fells and north-west of the Earl's seat. There was a river there too, the Endrick Water, and not far to the west, less than twelve miles away, Loch Lomond. Killearn estate was exceptional both as a shooting estate and for its fine oaks growing on a good clay loam. Its ash trees too were good, producing straight grain eagerly sought after by carriage makers and the like. Its fine conifers went to the shipyards of the Clyde to make tall stays, the cradles in which the hulls of great battleships were built.

They looked at the countryside and sighed for the milder climate of the Ayrshire coast, for the banks and braes of Doon, and the friends they had in Alloway and Maybole, but this nostalgia for Ayrshire soon passed. A summer went, a winter, and a spring, and Jane Shaw told her husband that their sixth child was on the way. This time they hoped for a girl. Five strapping boys might delight a man's heart, but one girl was surely not too much to ask for. In due course William Shaw's hopes were realised, and Jeannie Shaw was born in 1901. The family knew little joy that year and for long after, however, for Jane Shaw died in giving birth to her daughter. A cousin had to be summoned from Glasgow to take charge of the family. William had his work in the woods of Killearn and round about the Colonel's estate, where there was always more to be done than could be achieved in a working day, in the week, the month, or the year. He found it hardly mattered that the house that had been promised poor Jane began to take shape. The boys did many things for themselves that their mother had always done for them. He soldiered on, and time took care of his grief so that only now and again he felt sadness at the thought of their early days at Kilkerran and Doonholm. No one, man or woman, can live with the dead. When Jeannie, the baby of the family, was five years old, William Shaw married again.

It takes a very understanding woman to make a good stepmother to a ready-made close-knit family. The new Mrs Shaw did her best. If the surest way to a man's heart was through his stomach Mrs Shaw tried to win the hearts of her stepsons and stepdaughter, but she occupied the

boys with whatever tasks had to be done about the new
house. They gathered the eggs, cleaned the henhouse and
the cowshed. They carried wood, peeled potatoes and fed
the pig. They rose early and sat quietly reading when their
father came home tired at night. James had a bicycle which
he rode when he had finished his daily tasks and his schoolwork. Sometimes when the factor came to look over that
part of Killearn estate James surrendered his bicycle to
him and received a sixpence by way of reward. Money had
never been plentiful. The odd penny to buy such things
as *Sexton Blake*, *Union Jack* or *Boy's Realm* was hard to
come by. In trying to make a penny or two the Shaw boys
discovered what seemed a gold mine. Donald McEwan, the
licensed grocer's vanman who trundled about the countryside delivering groceries, ales, and the product of the
distillery, offered ninepence for a dozen empty half-
mutchkin whisky bottles, and a shilling and sixpence for a
dozen five-gill bottles. To gather so many whisky bottles
required a knowledge of human weaknesses and behaviour.
One of the boys, studying the Irish labourers on their way
back from a spree in Killearn or one of the neighbouring
places, noticed that when they had drunk from their
bottles they would toss them over the hedge. What better
place to earn a shilling than walking the hedgeside looking,
not for the nest of the linnet or the yellowhammer, but the
Glenlivet label on a half-mutchkin? Saturday night was a
good time for a carousel. Sunday morning would be a good
time to search, but if the penitents were at Mass that
morning, the sons of Shaw were at the kirk and not daring
even to whistle a tune on the way home! On Monday
morning they made search and gathered their harvest of
bottles, hiding them in a place safe from the eyes of those
who might have instigated a similar trade with Mr
McEwan. Carefully they would count their collection of
mutchkins (five gills weren't commonly carried back to
the bothy by the labourers working on roads, bridges or
dams in Stirlingshire) and estimate how long it would be

before they could carry them to the vanman and receive their reward. In the meantime they would drain all the bottles of such dregs as they might contain, keeping the 'blended' whisky in one of the bottles for a special bit of fun at home.

The old poachers often talked of catching pheasants by feeding them mash into which they had poured whisky. It seemed to the boys that a collection of drunk hens would provide as much amusement as anything they could think of and they surreptitiously stole a slice or two of bread and 'doctored' it with their hoarded whisky. The hens flocked round them, bolting down the well-soaked bread the boys threw to them. The cockerels took more than their share! Soon it was obvious that the henrun was like Killearn when the labourers were celebrating. Hens staggered and fell down flapping. The cockerels faced up to each other and fought away, sometimes drawing blood and sometimes tumbling.

'Look at that!' the boys shouted with delight as the intoxicated hens fell about.

The Shaws kept a large flock and there was barely enough whisky-soaked bread to satisfy the demand! William Shaw, coming in at the gate, paused and listened to the sounds of merriment.

'What are those boys up to now?' he asked his wife.

Mrs Shaw shook her head and looked a little grim. 'I'm sure I don't know but it will be some mischief!'

William Shaw edged his way round the corner of the house and stood gaping at the scene that met his eyes. The boys were quite helpless with laughter. The hens were equally helpless. A grin broke on William Shaw's face. He tried to hide it, but in a minute he found himself laughing. Mrs Shaw joined him and gasped with indignation.

'My birds! My poor hens! What have you been doing to them?'

'We only gave them a drop of whisky,' said one of the boys lamely. 'It'll not do them any harm, will it?'

'Flavour their eggs, I shouldn't wonder,' said their father. 'Who would want whisky-flavoured eggs?'

'The Irishmen,' said James.

It was suddenly quite clear to William Shaw how the boys had obtained the whisky. He wiped his eyes and looked at his wife before he delivered his verdict.

'Now there will be no more draining old whisky bottles to make your mother's birds drunk! You hear me? It's cruel. It's wicked and you should never do such a thing to an animal!'

He tried to avoid looking at the cock of the walk as that once dignified and vain bird collided with a hencoop and fell off his feet.

'You hear what I say?'

The Shaw boys looked at one another and bowed their heads to hide their grins.

'I will give you each a leathering if I ever catch you doing this again! Now get in the house and sit you there for an hour as a punishment!'

The boys filed past their father and went indoors. It was a week before they succumbed a second time and stole a larger lump of bread to go with an even larger quantity of whisky-bottle drainings. This time the hens came at speed, flying down the run to be sure of getting their share. The effect was as devastating as ever. The cocks squared up to one another and fell down in frustration. The hens went their ways like old drunken crones leaving a gin parlour. Mrs Shaw stood at the window and resolved that her husband should deal with the crime as he had promised. It wasn't often that the Shaw boys got a leathering. The taws, almost an exact replica of the schoolmaster's belt, hung by the mantelpiece. It served more as a warning than an instrument of punishment, but this time the boys had gone too far! If the hens laid again it would be a wonder, Mrs Shaw told herself. They were more likely to drown in the drinking trough or get jammed somewhere under the hen-house and die there.

The punishment came as inevitably as nightfall. William Shaw was not given to idle threats. He believed in fun of a proper kind, and everything in its proper place, but getting hens drunk seemed to be in danger of becoming a habit in the family, and he couldn't have that!

'It's your turn, James,' he said. 'Stand you there, Gilbert. You're next, and then you, Robert!'

The taws rose and fell and justice was done.

At school James wasn't treated to the taws as often as some of the others. He worked hard at the three R's and Mr Alexander Stephens spared him punishment, even when he arrived some time after the bell had rung. His nickname was 'Lateboy' but this he couldn't help, for it was the burden of his stepmother's chores that kept him late. The girls of the school had a more endearing name for him. They called him Jim Crow and he blushed to hear it, because there had been howls of laughter at his imitation of a 'cushat' or pigeon which everyone had thought more like the croak of the crow. Jim Crow he was for the rest of his school days. There is no escaping a well-earned nickname.

While he worked his way from the infant section of the one-roomed village school through the junior section to what was known as the 'big end', young Jim Shaw harboured a secret ambition. It was to work out of doors, to be a forester and plant trees. As a small child he had walked about the garden at Doonholm sticking twigs in the soft loam and imitating his father.

'Look at that wee boy,' his mother would say. 'You can tell he's going to be a woodman!'

William Shaw had laughed. He had never thought of any of the family following in his own footsteps. It didn't signify anything that his own father and grandfather had been woodmen. A woodman's life was hard. It was a business a boy shouldn't be put into, but enter of his own free will if ever he did so at all. Young Jim was the only one to want the life it might seem, but Jim was only a boy and time would tell. There were surely other and easier ways of making a living.

Mr Stephens might have agreed. He knew that 'Jim Crow' wanted to leave school at the earliest opportunity and he wasn't included in the group who were being schooled for higher education in such subjects as Latin and French, but he had appointed Jim 'censor' or marker of the lower section of the 'big end'. Sitting apart, the woodman's son lent an ear to accounts of the Gallic Wars and Latin verbs. Sometimes, when the star pupils failed him, Mr Stephens would turn to Jim Crow and demand an answer. Jim Crow was often able to construe as required, much to the schoolmaster's delight.

'There!' he would exclaim. 'And this is a boy who isn't supposed to be paying attention! This is a boy who isn't taking Latin at all!'

Mr Stephens waylaid the head woodman when he got an opportunity.

'Mr Shaw,' he said, 'I have been thinking about that boy of yours, young James. It seems to me that he could go a lot further and do a lot better with a little encouragement. The three R's are all very well, but a boy who is willing and able to learn, as James proves he is sitting there listening to the others, could maybe get a Marshall Trust Bursary. His education wouldn't cost a penny more. He could fit himself for better things. What do you think of putting him to?'

William Shaw scratched his head and frowned. He was essentially practical in his outlook.

'What a man really likes doing, he does best. What James wants to do is what matters. I will talk to him. I'll tell him what you have mentioned to me. It will be up to the boy. I can't say more than that.'

That night William Shaw took the copy of *Union Jack* young Jim was reading and laid it on one side.

'Now boy,' he said, 'Mr Stephens was talking to me about you today. There is the question of what you are

going to do with yourself, what way you are going to earn
your living, and whether you are going on at school or
leaving maybe next year. Now if you want school it's up
to you. It's your life and you have a say in what's to be
done.'

'I want to be a forester,' said Jim Crow. 'I want that and
nothing else. I want to leave school. I don't want to work
for a bursary, supposing I was certain I could get one! I
want to leave and work in the forest like you!'

William Shaw shook his head. He hadn't wanted such a
vehement declaration. He knew that James had no wish
to remain at school, but working in the wood was another
matter. He had striven hard and long in estate service.
Not everyone who went into the wood emerged a head
woodman and became the right hand of his master. There
were only so many forest estates in Scotland and only so
many opportunities to become head forester. The railway,
on the other hand, was a respectable calling with opportunities for diligent, hard-working youngsters seeking to
climb the tree and become managers.

'We'll have to see, James,' he said. 'We're not deciding
what you're going to do, just what you're not going to do.
If you don't want to work at the schoolwork that's all
right, but we've a wee while yet, and time to make up our
minds about the road you'll travel.'

Young Jim Crow's heart sank. He knew without being
told that his father was opposed to him going into the
wood and becoming a forester. Almost certainly he would
make him take a job in the service of the North British
Railway.

'I don't want to be a railway clerk or even an engine
driver,' he said to himself. 'I want to work out of doors in
the forest and if I can't be that, I'll be nothing!'

He was a very determined youngster, but William
Shaw was an equally determined man.

2

Escape from the Desk

In the railway age the sound of trains rumbling through the quiet countryside at five or six o'clock in the morning had become a sort of herald of the day, more reliable than the lark or even the first streaks of light combed on the sky to the east. The sound of the morning train depressed young Jim Shaw in July 1907 for he knew then that his fate was sealed. He was promised to the railway, and his future would almost certainly be polishing the seat of his trousers on an office stool. The ring of the telegraph might sound exciting when a boy stood on the station on a wild night and someone was reporting trouble on the line up around Aberfoyle, or over towards Balloch on Loch Lomond where the mist had crept down off the hills, but who wanted to man a telegraph? Who wanted to perch at a desk looking out at the station yard with nothing more exciting coming his way than a few bundles of shot or snared rabbits being consigned to Glasgow by the Killearn keeper, or a sack of potatoes on its way to some farmer's poor relative in Govan?

'You'll stick in and make a good thing of this job. There's a big future on the railway,' William Shaw told his son. Mr Shaw had been busy telling the station master that young Jim was industrious and a good lad, and he was, after all, the son of a man in authority, the Colonel's forester. Respectability was essential on the North British. A lad couldn't get anywhere without it. Respectability and responsibility went hand in glove, and being in charge of the entry of weigh bills and dockets, which piled up under a paper-weight on the steep slope of the ink-stained desk, was responsibility. How could things ever get to Aberfoyle or Balloch, or even down the road a bit to Dumgoyne, where there was a distillery, without someone like Jim Shaw to sit making his entries in the book and spiking the bills after he had entered them? The very smell of the place was the smell of commerce—the smell of earthy sacks and Archangel tar, sisal rope and cheese. The sound was equally unexciting, the clank of iron, the clucking of crated pullets, the yelping of a pup being consigned to someone in the Highlands to the north. How could anyone compare this to the scents and sounds of the forest? How could anyone rest easy in such a prison?

'How did you like it then?' he was asked by his stepmother after that first wearisome July day.

Jim looked up at the green leaves of the trees and listened to the sound of a crosscut being used by someone not far away. If his stepmother expected him to say he liked it fine she was going to be disappointed.

'I suppose it's like that in Barlinnie,' he said.

Mrs Shaw knew it was useless to tell Jim that he was tired. That it would be better tomorrow, and what happened on the railway could be exciting.

'I suppose you answered the telegraph?' she asked.

'Aye,' he said. 'I answered it. Somebody at Aberfoyle asked me if I was Mr William Shaw's son. I said I was. He said, "Lad, I don't know what you want sitting in a stinking office on a summer's day like this, when you could be helping your father in Craighat wood!" He was somebody from Killearn. He didn't say his name.'

'Early to bed then,' said his stepmother. 'You've to be there at seven.'

He went to bed, but it was a long time before he

managed to get to sleep. It was a dull world. His life was as dull as it would have been had he stayed on with the other pupils and tried for a bursary.

In the morning, however, he escaped, if only for an hour. Here, all at once, was relief from the dreary entries and the ringing of the bell. Here was something more interesting than the endless gossip between stations, and the idle talk of the people who called with their parcels.

'Telegram for Mrs Wilson at Aucheneck House,' said the station-master, cum-senior clerk cum-ticket collector. 'Haste you up there with it! I think it's important. Maybe you'll get a sixpence.'

In a minute he was off like a hare for the woodland path to Aucheneck House and freedom. He didn't stop until he was almost out of breath, but then he lay down on a grassy bank and put his hands beneath his head and stared up at the trees and the sky. He was free, and it seemed certain that this wouldn't be his one and only escape. There were bound to be more telegrams to be delivered, more urgent messages delivered when the bell rang in the office and someone had something to be read over. After a rest he got to his feet and hurried on. Deliver the telegram and then take time to loiter in the wood! He could always run back afterwards.

Mrs Wilson read the message and smiled at him.

'Good news,' she said. 'Now I must give you something.'

William Shaw's boy knew how to behave. He already had his cap off. He didn't hold out his hand for sixpence but waited for it to be offered. Mrs Wilson had no intention of offering him money, however. She signalled him to follow and went through to the kitchen.

'Give Master Shaw a bag of sugar buns,' she told her cook.

Jim was a growing lad and buns were almost as welcome as pennies. He expressed his thanks and hurried away to find a seat beneath a great beech tree in the wood where he sat until he had eaten and savoured the very last crumb of his reward. It was time to get back, however. He sprang to his feet and ran for all he was worth back to Killearn Station.

'Well, James?' asked the station-master. 'Did you get a sixpence?'

'A bun,' he said, 'but it was a delicious bun.'

He would have been ashamed to confess that he had eaten a whole bag of buns. The next time he went to Aucheneck House it was a bowl of raspberries, the time after, strawberries. He had many an orgy of fruit-eating that summer. Aucheneck, like some of the other country houses in the locality, had a wonderfully well-stocked fruit garden and orchard. When he wasn't gorging himself on dessert gooseberries or plums, he was eating pears or apples, and he liked nothing better than fruit unless it was to be free in the woods. He solved the problem of utilising his time to the best end by a standing arrangement with his brother to borrow his bicycle so that he could deliver a telegram quickly. He didn't hurry back. It was extraordinary how often that bicycle managed to get a puncture on the last stage of a journey

Fruit gorging was to prove his undoing, however, for one day when he sat down to demolish a particularly large bounty of William pears he quite forgot the passing of time. The corn had been cut, the world was golden, drowsy, blessed by the soft light of the autumn sun. The juice of the pears ran down the truant's chin. Time went in endless, unrecorded minutes until far away a train whistle reminded Jim that he was late, very late! He threw himself on the bicycle, stretched his long legs and pedalled for all he was worth. At the first bend the hard road almost ripped the sole from his boot as he tried to steady himself. At the next bend there was no saving anything. Over the hedge and through barbed wire on top of a fence, and down in a whirl of wheels and jingling loose parts. Jim was bruised and cut. The bicycle was a wreck! Worse than the disaster to the machine or his own cuts and bruises was the fact that time had run out. Only a miracle could get him to Killearn in time! He was suddenly inspired to run with the wrecked bicycle to Dumgoyne Station, leave it there with the request that it be sent up the line to Killearn in due course, and race on for all he was worth to be at his desk when the train came in! The train was just reaching Killearn when he ran in and sat down.

'Well, boy,' said the station-master, 'you seem out of breath?'

'A wee bit,' he admitted, his chest heaving.

'Out of breath! A wonder the lad's not got a broken neck, the way he came down that hill at Dumgoyne on his bike.'

Jim looked with dismay at Jim Paul, the market-gardener who had come in with a great package of flowers he wanted sending on to Glasgow.

The station-master raised his eyebrows. 'What bike?' he asked.

'My brother's bike,' Jim confessed. 'You see I can deliver the telegrams quicker on a bike.'

'And what do you do with the time you save, Master Shaw?'

Jim flushed and bowed his head to his work.

'Mind you, Jim,' said the station-master, who was a kindly man, 'you must buckle to. Soon, if there's a good report on you, you'll be off out of here, to Stirling or some-where like that! They've got no less than four telegraphs at Stirling. Busy all the time. No chance to go begging buns or eating rasps from the hedge when you're there, and then maybe you'll go on to Berwick and be manager of the line one day, top man of the whole North British even!'

Jim went home that evening breathing the scents of autumn, his heart heavier than it had been on his first day. Stirling and then maybe Berwick!

'And why not?' asked his stepmother. 'Many a man

has gone to the top with less of a start than you have. Think of Carnegie!'

He didn't think of Carnegie. He thought of the woods and lads of his own age sitting eating their dinner round a fire of bark and splinters and maybe watching a squirrel leaping from the furthermost branch of one tree, through the air like an acrobat, to land on the next. Didn't anyone think about Jim Shaw, the prisoner behind the booking-office window?

When he went out into the wood he listened to the owls calling to one another across miles and miles of woodland that included Killearn and many another shadowed mansion tucked away in the heart of a forest.

'I will not stop!' he said to himself, but he stayed. A sense of obligation to his father and the efforts he had made to get him a job with the North British made him stick at it through the autumn, the winter and spring. The following summer recognition of the sort he dreaded came to him. He was posted to Stirling.

'Stirling,' said his stepmother. 'Now there's a place! Think of being in Stirling. There's Stirling Castle and, and . . . '

'The cattle yard,' said William Shaw whose feet were firmly on the ground as always. 'The cattle yard means that the railway is twice as busy. I'm told they operate four telegraphs there.'

'Well,' said Jim, 'they won't get me delivering the telegrams all over Stirling. They can get somebody else to do that!'

There were roars of laughter at this but Jim saw nothing funny about any of it. His day would be from eight o'clock in the morning until eight o'clock at night. He would be paid the magnificent sum of £30 a year, or eleven shillings and sixpence ha'penny a week. They had found him lodg-ings with a Mrs Gow in Bruce Street where his immediate superior already lodged. His bed and board would be ten shillings and sixpence and his laundry ninepence,

which even if he hadn't been the brightest boy at arithmetic anybody who could count at all knew left threepence ha'penny to play with!

'She's a good, kind-hearted woman, they tell me,' said
William Shaw, 'and you'll get a free trip home on the train
every weekend if you want to come.'

If he wanted to come! The dread of going to Stirling
would have been unbearable had there been no chance to
come back again to Killearn whenever he wanted to come.

His bag was packed and he set off on the train on a
Sunday to be in time for his first day at the station office on
Monday at eight o'clock. Mrs Gow proved to be a motherly
soul. The food she served was good. She washed his clothes
and mothered him. He was introduced to Duncan Grey,
under whom he would work at Stirling Station; ah, but he
was a pale-faced townsman, a pen-pusher. The world
seemed to be made up of men who worked and men who
recorded, men who toiled with the axe and the saw, and
men who noted it down. The desk was all right for a man
who wanted to sit down for the rest of his life and lie in a
coffin at the end, but Jim Shaw wanted none of that, nor
could he get excited about Aberdeen when it sounded
no different from the bell ringing for Aberfoyle. The
messages were much the same. The bills and transactions
were exactly the same, only longer and perhaps more
complicated. They sat late 'cashing' up. No one said
'Here's a bag of buns for you, James Shaw' or gave him
a William pear, although they were supposed to grow
even better fruit in that part of the world than at Killearn.

'I'm not going to stick it, Mr Grey,' he said. 'It's not
for me!'

Mr Grey shook his head. 'Lad,' he said, 'you've a good
report behind you. You could be on your way to North
Berwick. You could be . . . '

'Manager of the whole North British! I know. My stepmother and my father have told me. All I want to do is to
be in the wood and use a saw and an axe. I want to plant

trees and work a sawmill! I want to grow trees and see ships made with them. I want the fresh air. I don't want the old stale smell of bacon and hides from the tannery and bundles of newspapers and rows of creamery cans like soldiers. I want to be free.'

Mr Grey took this as some sort of criticism of himself. 'We all want to be free and do what we like, James Shaw, but in this life we can't do as we like!'

For six weeks the telegraph rang. For six weeks James worked through the lunch hour to relieve his senior colleague. For six weeks he ate his heart out and wandered about, wondering how he would be greeted when he gave up the railway and returned home, for this is what he was determined to do. Life was only bearable even when his father gave him the extra half-crown to see him through the week. No matter what attraction there might be for the dedicated stool-perching railway clerk in the distant prospect of North Berwick and the seat of power, Jim Shaw's heart was at home, creeping into the woods like the roe deer and listening to the vastness of its near silence.

'Well then, Mrs Gow,' he said on Sunday morning when he left. 'Thank you for being so good to me. I'm not coming back. Goodbye, Mr Grey. Tell them I'm very sorry but I can't stick it any longer. I suppose they might ask for a week's notice, but you tell them I've worked late and done all that you asked me to do. I'm at the end of it now.'

'Goodbye then, James Shaw. I hope you get what you want. Not many boys do, and a lot would be glad of the chance you've had.'

'I know,' he said and carried his bag down to the station, happy but anxious at the same time.

There was no disguising the fact that he hadn't just come home on an overnight visit, but had given up his employment with the North British Railway, for he had brought his things and the tie was severed. William Shaw

looked hard at young Jim. Well, the boy had never pretended that he liked working for the railway. He was home
again. His elder brothers had been happy enough, one
going for engineering, one to landscape gardening and
Gilbert destined to become a sergeant one day in the Ayr
Police. Jim, it seemed, had the bit between his teeth.

'What now then?' Mr Shaw asked, knowing the answer
before he heard it spoken.

'I'm not going back,' said Jim. 'I told Duncan Grey and
Mrs Gow.'

'You had no right to leave the way you have done! They
are entitled to some consideration. You should give notice!
What will anybody else who takes you on think, knowing
that you up and left the North British without giving
notice?'

Young Jim bowed under the reprimand. He hadn't,
after all, been the General Manager of the railway, or
even its senior booking clerk at Stirling! He had done all
they asked of him while he had worked there, and more
besides, for he had hung on with Duncan Grey while they
worked out the cash and tallies day after day.

'I want to work with you in the wood,' he said.

William Shaw nodded thoughtfully.

'I can't take you on to work in the wood unless I talk to
the Factor. Am I to tell him you leave when you think
you will?'

'I'll work hard,' said Jim.

'Anybody that works for me works hard,' his father
said, not unkindly, 'and keeps working.'

Mrs Shaw found him a chore to do almost at once. She
knew that the Factor would be up from Ayr in due time.
He wouldn't come just because James Shaw wanted work.
He would come when estate business required him to
come. In the meantime James would moon and mess
about doing nothing. He had to be kept to some kind of
discipline!

Young Jim was only too pleased to do whatever his

stepmother wanted. He was relieved that his desertion of the North British had been finally forgiven. Now it was only a matter of time before someone got him a job in the wood. He went to hoe and tidy the garden. He scraped the potatoes he had dug, sitting on a chair at the back door and dropping them into a big iron pot half-full of water. He fed the pig, and cleaned the cowshed, wheeling the dung to the midden. He was a paragon of industry and he loved every minute of his freedom, for it was a long time since he had spent days on end out of doors. The distant hills were blue with heather bloom. The air was rich with the scent of honeysuckle draping the hedge, and no matter what happened, this was where he was going to work, outside in the shade of trees, broad, leafy oaks, tall, towering larches and pines, broad-based Norway spruces underneath which pheasants ran to shelter.

'Well,' said his father, spooning milk on to his porridge at breakfast time. 'The Factor is with us today.'

Young Jim could hardly eat his breakfast. Today he would know! At dinner-time his father came home and sat down to the table before he spoke.

'Mr Johnson wants to see you at the House this afternoon. You'll go up at three.'

They finished their meal and Jim went to get washed. It was a long time before the Factor would receive him, but he wanted to be ready. At three o'clock he went smartly up to the door of the House and rang the bell. There was a long pause. He hesitated and thought to ring it again, but then he heard a footfall on the flags within and took off his cap and waited.

'Well, James Shaw!' said one of the maids. 'Do you know this is the front door? Do you not know you're supposed to knock at the back door?'

'Mr Johnson sent for me,' he said.

'Indeed! Well, you better come in then.'

The more menial a servant was the more intolerant they seemed to be, for the Factor himself greeted the boy with a great deal more sympathy. 'Good afternoon, Master Shaw,' he said. 'I understand from your father that you want to be employed on the Colonel's staff?'

It was a grand way of asking him if he really wanted to work in the wood, but Jim said that he did.

'I expect you know what it would mean, James? You would work for half a crown a week for three years. You would be shown everything and taught everything that might fit you to be a woodman, a forester like your father, in due time. Whenever there might be courses that would benefit you you would be sent on them. You would be expected to read and educate yourself in forestry and sylviculture. At such times as the Home Farm needed help at hay or harvest you would be available to help, and you would, on those occasions, get another one shilling and sixpence a week. Do you think this is what you want?'

Jim said it was, all he wanted.

'If I can help you in any way you must write to me at Ayr, or ask to see me when I am at Killearn. Your father will arrange it. If you work hard there is no telling where you may go. Your father's father was a woodman and I believe your grandfather's father too.'

As he plodded back down to his father's house young Jim's heart sang. At last, at last, he had escaped from the school and the railway office. He would never go back to either!

'Well,' said his stepmother, 'did you impress Mr Johnson?'

'I think so,' he said hopefully. 'He didn't say when I was to start. I wanted to ask him that but I didn't like to.'

The question was answered that night when his father came home.

'Tomorrow morning you'll be down at the toolshed at seven o'clock with the men. You'll have a piece with you because you won't be coming home at dinnertime. You're starting work and you'll be like any other boy working on the estate, except you'll behave better. You'll remember that you're my son. If I have to punish one boy I'll punish them all and you won't get off, so mind you that, Jim.'

Jim nodded and got off to bed after his 'piece'—in this case a roast-beef sandwich—had been made up. He was filled with excitement as he thought of himself swinging an axe and felling one of the giant conifers destined for the shipyard.

In the morning he was out and away before his father. At the toolshed he joined the woodmen and apprentices.

'Look who's here!' they said. 'Jim Shaw the pen-pusher from the railway! What made you give it up, Jim? Weren't they going to make you General Manager at Stirling or somewhere?'

He laughed with them. 'Berwick,' he said, 'but the money wasn't good enough. I thought I might as well come home and start at the bottom again. I'll be happy enough cutting down trees.'

They winked at each other as he stepped forward and helped himself to an axe. The trained staff had their own axes, which were personal tools, as were hedgeknives and saws. A number of axes were available for use by the second- and third-year apprentices but Jim had set his heart on tree-felling that day. He was allowed to step out of the shed with the chosen axe and join the group who were waiting to be sent to the conifer wood. Mr Shaw came on the scene at that moment and quickly delegated the foreman to see that men went to their respective tasks.

'Where do you think you're off to, my lad?' he asked young Jim.

'I'm off to cut the larches,' said Jim hopefully.

He knew at once from his father's face that no such excitement was to be his. Mr Shaw spoke over his shoulder.

'My boy wants to learn forestry,' he said. 'The best place to begin is at the beginning, in the nursery, so you'll set him to weeding the nursery plots, Davy!'

The seedling ash trees in the nursery plot were between eighteen and twenty inches high. Growing among them were dandelions and docks that threatened to choke them. Jim gazed with dismay at the sight as he buckled on the leather knee-pad and took the three-pronged weeding tool Andrew Buchanan, the foreman, gave him in exchange for the axe. It was a less bright day than yesterday had been. In fact the sky had turned a leaden colour. Hardly had he begun to prod the roots of the tenacious dandelions and docks than it began to hail. It hailed off and on all day. The boy's hands became so cold that they turned blue and he was near to tears. He didn't pause to think that he had been earning at least four times as much sitting on a stool in Stirling, and would have been paid more in a year or so! He weeded out the dandelions and docks and laid them lengthwise in a basket so that his taskmaster could see that he had pulled the whole root and left none in the heavy clay of the nursery bed. It would be a year before they put an axe in his hand, and he was beginning to understand why his father said it was no easy life. It took a day and a half to weed 500 square yards of ash seedlings and another 500 square yards of beech and oak awaited him after that. At five o'clock, when his back seemed to be set in a permanent crick, he straightened up and took himself home. He had to work a month before he received his wages in the form of a half-sovereign or two bright new crowns. From this sum his father would return to him twopence or threepence with which he might buy sweets or broken biscuits at the little shop in Killearn.

When the weeding chore was over the newcomer found that he had been admitted to the fraternity of the apprentices. He enjoyed their dinner-time horse-play as much as they did and took part in competitions and displays of strength with which they entertained their elders. The older woodmen took a delight in encouraging the boys to compete. There was potato-splitting, for instance, which demonstrated accuracy with a hedgeknife. The potato, thrown in the air, had to be cut with a horizontal slash of the knife which sent the two pieces flying, one up, and the other down. A boy who was really quick and accurate could get in another cut at either of the two pieces. The chopped potatoes were compared for size and neatness of cut. A small pool of pennies went to the apprentice judged the winner. When potato-slashing palled there was matchstick-splitting with a six-pound axe. This was demonstrated by laying the matchstick on a flat stump and swinging the axe to slit the matchstick neatly down its length. An extra prize could be earned by not simply letting the heavy axe fall, as some apprentices did, but by swinging in the traditional manner, across the hip. This required particular co-ordination of arm and eye and was not easily done even by an expert.

A more nerve-testing competition was tree-sliding. This was done on one of the individually planted Norway spruces which had never been dressed, but allowed to grow in its natural pyramid form from tip to ground level, the tree being perhaps thirty feet at the base and sixty feet in height. A boy would climb up through the branches until he reached the tip of the tree and there, at a given signal, jump off. The stout branches of the tree would take his weight and as he slid down one of the old hands would check on his watch how many seconds the descent had taken. The boy who reached the ground in the shortest time won the kitty!

Young Jim climbed his first spruce and stood like a sailor at the masthead, waiting to be told to jump. The sea of faces seemed far below. The wood stretched out like a great green carpet on either side. This was what every apprentice in the wood did. This was a test of his head for heights, essential in a tree-feller. This was the moment. The hand of the man with the watch waved. He sprang off and came down with what seemed the speed of the falcon stooping. There was nothing to it! After a little practice he was able to win the kitty. He enjoyed going aloft and coming back down in a tenth of the time it had taken to climb up.

Going through the plantation of young trees, helping to clear the trash and weeds in the narrow lanes between them, young Jim discovered here and there an ash with a bend at the root, a natural walking stick which, when it could be surreptitiously extracted, would sell for six-pence. One of the older apprentices showed him how to make even better crook handles from ash saplings by tying the root round a draining tile. A shepherd might part with two and sixpence or more for a good crook-handled ash stick. The thing was to remember where the stick was being 'grown' into a crook. This could be done by marking the fence at the end of the row and walking the row a year or so later. A great trade in whips could be done with the ostler at the Glasgow contractors of Wordie and Co. who paid sixpence or ninepence for beech sticks of five feet or so in length. These, with a thong of leather at the end, made whips for the carters. Coachmen, too, paid well for a suitable holly stick of eight or nine feet. These were much favoured for whips. Long holly sticks were hard to find, however. They tended to grow on the edges of gorges or steep gullies. Many a woodman trying to earn himself a few extra shillings fell and injured himself trying to cut a holly stick from a dangerous place. Occasionally men were killed doing this.

Apart from thinning and pruning, and the harvest work for the Home Farm, young Jim found himself occupied from Bank Holiday almost until Christmas, if not in the woods themselves, out on the estate roads, trimming hedges. The fine thorn and beech hedges of Kil-learn weren't 'laid' as in the southern part of Britain, but shorn of their annual growth and tapering from the base of the hedge. While this work was being done the apprentice would draw attention to any gaps or holes in the hedges so that these could be 'filled in' at planting time from November to March. Pride in this work was a sign of the *esprit de corps* of the Killearn estate. Men engaged on the work were keen to ensure that neighbouring estates never outdid them in neatness and evenness of trimming and when the Colonel drove to visit his friends he could see that he was well served.

3

The Tree-Planter

THERE was little or no glamour to what an apprentice
had to do in the woods. True, he saw much more than a
boy who was kept out of the woods by the gamekeepers
and woodmen. Roe deer walked the glades and falcons
sailed and stooped to kill their prey while, now and again,
an old fox paused with paw upraised and looked boldly
back at the lads who had disturbed him. On winter
mornings a coldness never left the deep shadows of the
wood. The bark of old trees would be touched with frost
until a watery sunlight penetrated to melt it away. In
spring it might be more comfortable, but in summer there
were the flies endlessly breeding among the bracken and
the ferns. It was some compensation to come upon the
nest of a bird or catch a rabbit with his hands, but Jim
Shaw was in the woods to learn his trade. He needed an
instructor, someone who would give him all his attention
when he had questions to be answered.

What Davy Carr told young Jim about trees and tree-
planting had a special sort of magic about it because Davy
was steeped in wood-lore. He lived in the wood as another
man might have lived in his stable or a priest in an abbey.
Trees, to the old senior forester, were a monument set in
place for another generation to admire. Mature trees, such
as the giant beech and the oak, were a link with a man's

ancestors. Anyone who planted was benefiting mankind in general.

'Aye be planting a tree,' he told Jim. 'It will be growing when you are sleeping.'

This piece of wisdom had a particular depth of meaning. An oak tree may grow for a hundred and fifty years to reach maturity. Even the less substantial sycamore doesn't reach its prime in less than sixty years, although an ash will generally be harvested long before it attains such an age.

'Aye be planting a tree,' the red-bearded Perthshire man said. The boy remembered. He waited upon Davy Carr, who was one of his father's privileged right-hand men. He listened to everything that old Davy said as though Davy had newly come from receiving the word of God on the mountain. He worshipped him as a boy often worships an old man. The two worked and walked and talked together at every opportunity. When it was time for Davy to get his hay from the woods, a perk which he enjoyed because of his special position on the Killearn estate, young Jim was among the most willing of the recruits sent to help. Davy needed the hay for his cow. There wasn't enough pasture to keep the cow milking and to supply hay from the small field he had on the outskirts of the village. The woodmen set to and helped scythe grass from open ground and banks within the perimeter of the wood. When enough had been cut it was raked and turned and finally gathered and carted. Young Jim worked hard and diligently to see that the ground he was allocated was thoroughly raked. When he carried what he had gathered he was careful to see that not a wisp was left behind. In return for this devotion Davy Carr instructed his favourite pupil.

'Look how a wood grows,' he would say, straightening his back and wiping the sweat from his brow. 'It is a wonderful design that seeds the beech in the shade while the oak and the ash need sunlight. You'll see how different are the oak and the fir tree if you lift them. The oak lives by its strong tap root and the conifer grows a fibrous surface root that spreads across shallow loam. It's easy to pull up a fir. If you pull it up and transplant it you do it good, for it grows an even more fibrous root and does better a year later. The oak doesn't care for transplanting. Its long root comes out as readily as an old wisdom tooth. It likes to grow where it has chosen to grow. The best oak is always the one that stands where the acorn fell and germinated. If it takes more than the lifetime of your old grandfather it is still the best hardwood!'

The fields of Killearn Home Farm that had been in rye-grass or timothy were cut and the crop stored away. The oats and barley too were stooked and built into ricks, before the tree-fellers were admitted to the woods where William Shaw had marked oaks. Davy Carr explained the wisdom of delaying the felling until well on in November. He and young Jim worked in the same locality as the merchants' men. The fellers were aware of this scrutiny even although they pretended otherwise. Their axes rose and fell with resounding thuds. Their saws rasped and twanged as they did their work. Oak chips and sawdust were sprinkled over a debris of dying leaves and acorns. A hundred yards away the teams stood munching in their nosebags, waiting to haul the dressed trunks out of the wood.

'Is it not a terrible mess they make?' asked the youngster as he and Davy sat eating their 'piece' and drinking their tea. 'Look at the way they have torn up the ground, trampling it and making a midden of it, like a badly ploughed field!'

Old Davy supped his tea and looked over at the fellers and the great oaks they had toppled. 'Trees come to their time,' he said. 'They are worth not so much if they go on. They are worth less if they are taken too soon. They are ripe and ready, and wages have to be paid. As for what they are doing, lad, your father is pleased to see them do it!

When the horses have hashed and bashed and torn and pulled, and the trunks have been dragged away, what has happened? Well, I'll tell you. Before they came anywhere near the place the acorns dropped. Your father wouldn't let them in until that happened. Now they trample them into the ground that grew the trees they came from, d'you see? They plough them in! They roll them in, thousands of the best acorns you could gather from any of the woods for miles around. Mark what I say, and look at this place later on. You can cut a tree when the sap is back down and sealed. Anybody will tell you that, but if a tree grows well in a place, and has good seed, and you can get it planted for you, that's perfect management. It takes three to six weeks for the acorns to germinate. Next summer you'll see what they have done for us today, maybe a hundred, maybe two hundred oaks, growing where we know they'll do well.'

Jim Shaw watched one of the fellers running a tape round an oak while another man made a note in a pocket-book. They were measuring the tree's girth. Merchants calculated on quarter girth for board cutting and paid the estate on this basis. They were satisfied with what they were getting—some fine, straight-grained Killearn oak. They didn't dream that they too were benefiting a generation to come by planting more oaks on the site. The Killearn oaks went for railway wagons, the furniture trade, and the shipbuilders. Beeches and sycamore, favoured by the wood turners, were used for making spindles, chair and table legs, rollers for mangles and cotton mills. Standing in the lines of old beech trees the young forester had his dreams. The beeches were like great, smooth-skinned elephants ruminating in the mellow sunlight. Beneath them a squirrel scampered about, pausing occasionally to store away food he would probably never uncover again.

That he might be planting trees he wouldn't see grow to seventy or eighty feet didn't occur to the apprentice. He was too busy. At this time he would call first thing in the morning to collect his seedlings at the nursery, packing them in his sack and carrying them on his back, as many as three or four hundred, depending upon the variety and the density of planting required. It was a tiring job. Often it rained. Sometimes the sun left the woodland early and a cold wind blew, but the tree-planters had their quota of planting to be done and they plodded on, however rough and uneven the ground. Beech seedlings would be planted at five-foot intervals. Oaks, because they were slower growing, four feet apart. Sometimes rows of oak were 'nursed' or sheltered by rows of conifer; the latter, rising quickly, forced the oaks to grow taller and then, in due time, the quickly-maturing conifers would be cut down. Larch was always needed about the estate where it was used for fences, gates, rustic work and that kind of thing.

The planter carried a long narrow spade with which he made a 'T'-shaped cut in the earth, prising up the turf to allow him to insert the seedling, and then firming it down again. When this operation was completed the measuring rod, an ash of four or five feet in length, was turned end over end and the planting repeated. Two sighting rods of roughly six feet marked the row and when a row was done the planter moved the rods and began again, going uphill and down, to plant oaks where oaks were called for, and beech where beech was to grow. Whenever a naturally-seeded tree of the species being planted was discovered in the row it was passed over. No one could establish a tree half so well as the naturally-germinated one. Here and there the planter occasionally came across another sort of growth known as a stool-shoot, and the forester would examine the shoots growing from the stump of some mature tree felled a year or two before. The less robust shoots would be struck out, and the strongest one left to grow on. Only the man with the axe, or perhaps the man on the sawbench, would know the stool-shoot tree when at last, in eighty or a hundred years or more, it was brought down. The axe would be turned as the feller swung it. The chip that came off would be warped and distorted. The man at the sawbench might notice a similar deformity at the broad end of the board, and perhaps ponder on the forester who had allowed that tree to regenerate.

Pruning was an equally important task that apprentices were set to in due season. A wood doesn't grow tall, compact and well-ordered on its own. Like a garden, its growth has to be cultivated and encouraged. Pruning is essential to both the size and the shape of the tree. Jim Shaw enjoyed this work almost as much as he enjoyed swinging an axe. Being sent to a particular toolshed to draw tools for his day's work on a particular occasion he lingered by the door for a minute or two, and the foreman asked him where he was going and what he was to do.

'I'm to go pruning the pines today,' he said, picking up the knife and making sure that it was sharp.

'Then look for Davy's watch!' said the foreman laughing.

An hour later, working away at his task, Jim noticed a sort of metallic ripple on the tree he was about to prune. He touched it and discovered that it was a watch-chain embedded in the sapling upon which it had been hung many years before. The tree had grown and 'swallowed' the chain. It had, he discovered with amazement, swallowed the watch as well, for protruding from the other side of the trunk was a third of the watch, and the remainder of the chain upon which it had been suspended. Taking to his heels the youngster ran to the toolshed for old Davy Carr and persuaded him to return with him to the place where he had found the watch. The old man could hardly believe his eyes. A good part of a lifetime had passed, and what remained of his watch reminded him of a warm day when, taking off his jacket, he had hung the watch for safety on that small sapling. There it was, locked up for ever in the grown tree. Not to waste time the old man had Jim cut the tree above and below the imprisoned watch. The section of the tree was taken away to be made into a desk ornament. Time waits for no man, they say, and a tree is a long time growing.

Whatever was done in the woods was noted by the head forester on his tours of inspection. Whatever was left undone or needed to be remedied was similarly noted. William Shaw would mark a tree that needed doctoring or surgery, involving some part of its branches or trunk being cut away. He would study the rabbit wire and the danger signals that told him defences were being penetrated by some unwanted creature, such as deer. Roe deer loved the woods. Only when their antlers were in velvet were they guilty of damage. It was estate practice to discourage the deer and keep their numbers within bounds, for if they didn't do a great amount of damage to the trees upon which they 'sharpened' their antlers, rubbing away the soft velvety covering that itched so much, tenants would object that roe, harboured in the woods, came out to plunder the crops, munching turnips and damaging ricks. Since roe deer are elusive by day, when they shelter in the woods, and almost impossible to detect or ambush by night, the estate would organise a drive and have the deer shot. The whole business provided excitement for the younger men and a sort of holiday for the older woodmen who took part in the ambush, fortifying themselves with a bottle of whisky, which cost something like five shillings at that time.

The roe deer moved by secret paths and weren't to be driven effectively except by keepers who knew their ways and woodmen familiar with every feature of the wild landscape. At first the ambush would have nothing to do but lie in some shady place, looking up at the trees, talking in whispers and passing the bottle, but then the deer would come. The guns would begin to break the silence of the afternoon as, one after another, roe deer ran headlong into death, tumbled, kicked and spilled their blood on the soft earth of the wood. Before it was over, the day would sicken even the wildest of the hunters. Anyone who wanted might have venison, a whole deer, a haunch or whatever joint or cut he fancied. The remainder would be hauled off to an old quarry and tumbled down into it. A charge of black powder encouraged a rockfall, and the slaughtered beasts were buried.

Old Davy Carr stood watching the deer being piled into the quarry after the last drive Killearn was to have, when his master came on the scene and joined him at the quarry's edge.

'You have destroyed a lot of deer today, Davy,' said the Colonel.

Old Davy didn't look up. 'I am thinking, Colonel,' he said, 'what a solemn thing is death.'

Colonel Blackburn cleared his throat, turned and went away. That he had been deeply moved was evident. The following day he stopped the head forester. 'Let the deer run, Willie,' he said. 'We'll have no more killing here! They do little harm and they don't deserve to be treated like this.'

William Shaw understood. 'As you wish, sir,' he said. 'I've felt that way myself for a long time now.'

The roe deer were spared from then on, but young Jim Shaw had one treasured memory of the killing time, a recollection of Sandy Patterson, the rabbit-catcher and water bailiff, who had, as usual, come to help with the thinning of the roe deer. It was the custom for each man who came to lay out his bottle of whisky to be passed round in general use by the whole company. The head keeper would bring a box of glasses into which the whisky would be poured as the bottle was passed. On this occasion the ritual came to a standstill because the glasses had been left behind. The thirsty men looked at one another, wondering if the supply would last when some were obviously bigger-mouthed than others and some had hands to which a bottle-neck stuck once it was tipped to the mouth.

'Hold on,' said the head keeper. 'There are still a few

old turnips in the field out there. We'll get some cut and hollowed out and they can serve as drinking cups.'

In a short time the turnips were pulled and brought to the wood. Those who weren't trimming turnips waited patiently for the task to be completed. Once the cups were fashioned the bottles followed one another round the circle like wooden horses on a roundabout. Never had whisky tasted so good, and never had they had such a great laugh! At length the keeper, hearing a whistle from the high woods, thought it time to post his guns in ambush. The beaters were coming down, plodding closer and closer to the part of the wood in which the guns were supposed to be distributed. The deer passed through, tossing their heads, swinging to right and to left, seeking what cover they could, but no shot greeted them. The silence of the wood was broken only by the brushing of branches, the tapping of the beaters' sticks on tree-trunks, the occasional sound of a whistle. Young Jim scratched his head. That the deer had managed to evade the guns was impossible, and yet not a shot had sounded! The head keeper was equally disturbed.

'Go carefully back in there, Jim Shaw, and find out what is wrong. Walk carefully, lad. I can't have you being shot for a deer. Ask them are they asleep or what!'

It was too late to do anything about the driven deer. They had gone on and might not be seen again until the spring, when they would be back, eating the shoots of nursery trees and fraying branches of ash and oak, from April until September and the rutting season.

Jim Shaw walked carefully. He knew what a charge from a muzzle-loader could do to a deer, and he knew about men who had tipped the bottle too often. He looked from side to side and whistled as he walked so that no one would take him for a roe deer. He came upon Sandy Patterson and gaped in wonderment for the tall, angular fellow was in a strange contortion. His legs had been crossed in a sort of plaited way and he was powerless to release them. He clutched his muzzle-loader and looked up at the youngster with relief.

'Oh laddie,' he gasped, 'laddie, get me loose! My legs are fankled! I canna get up.'

It was plain that something more than mere accident had caused Sandy to get his limbs so interlocked. He had, of course, taken his ease with the gun in his arms. Being the worse for wear, he had reclined so comfortably that his heels and toes had become fast. He couldn't rise when the time came to rise, nor could he prime and fire his gun. The deer had sniffed and run on. They knew a helpless man when they saw one!

Jim Shaw helped Sandy to his feet and supported him until he found the stiffness going from his legs.

'But not a shot was fired,' he told Sandy.

'They have all fallen asleep, I suppose,' said Sandy, a soft grin spreading over his weather-beaten face.

The youngster took his leave and went steadily on through the wood to complete the investigation. All the guns were lying inert with their backs against trees, or stretched full-length on the ground, but it seemed odd that although they had drunk some of the finest whisky from the best distilleries in the north, such well-seasoned whisky drinkers should have been incapacitated in this way. Jim shook each one and told him that the head keeper was waiting. They rose and made their way back, each staggering and lurching as he went. The head keeper, who had drunk from a little cup belonging to his pocket flask, shook his head and rubbed his chin.

'I can only think them old turnips were a bit rotten, fermented the way they get at this time of year. With their juice added to the whisky that was poured into them that brew must have been powerful stuff! I never in my life knew the like of this. We spent hours and never fired a shot!'

The sorry company of guns looked sheepish. It took several nips from someone's bottle, especially put on one side for a second occasion, before their spirits were completely restored, but this time there was no drinking from turnip cups.

While deer did little damage to the woods, rabbits, hares, squirrels, crows, magpies, rats and mice inflicted a toll upon the forester's work. Crows would root up seed and seedlings, searching for worms. Squirrels could kill conifers by chewing the tips of the trees in spring. Rabbits browsed on seedlings and the branch-tips of nursery trees. Hares left their teeth marks even higher up trees. Once rabbits penetrated the wire enclosure of a nursery or newly-planted area they established a warren. In a few weeks they bred up a colony that the rabbit-catcher might not be able to eliminate with all his cunning and all the help he could get. Jim Shaw was taught how to fence rabbits out of a planting and how to cope with those inside. He was taught to know his enemies, from the capercaillie, the old cock of the woods, to the crossbill, both of which did great harm to the conifer woods. While Sandy Patterson taught him how to recognise the track of a mole burrowing below ground, Davy Carr told him about the beetles, the may-bug or old bum-clock that buzzes about the woods and fields at twilight, the yellow wood-wasp that loves the silver fir and larch, the pine sawfly and the goat-moth, called the augur-worm because its caterpillar bores into the bark of the oak tree. Worse than these, the pine weevil that produces scabs on the pine and fir and lets the resin bleed away. That there were so many enemies might have daunted a novice, but Jim Shaw looked at forestry as a kind of farming, a continual battle with pests and predators, which, no matter how they bred up and infested trees, had to be won.

Withal, it was a healthy life. The air of the woods was clean and wholesome, good for the blood and the lungs. A pine wood's scent is almost intoxicating and there is something fresh and pure about a deciduous wood through which the breeze blows on a spring morning. In the autumn and often on cold winter days there would be the equally exhilarating scent of woodsmoke. Jim loved the burning of bark peelings and the wonderful smell of oak slowly smouldering in the heart of a fire. It was good to come home tired and catch a whiff of the burning wood from a neighbouring plantation. It made him feel alive, as he had never felt in the service of the railway company, and his tiredness would fall away and his step quicken in the hope that he might get out and play football before dark. He was a keen sportsman, interested in five-a-side football, which was popular in that part of Scotland in those times, as well as in athletics where he excelled as a runner.

Colonel Blackburn had been amused when he had been asked if his name might be taken by the five-a-side football team. They wanted to call themselves Blackburn Rovers, although it was unlikely that any of them had heard of an English professional team of that name. The Colonel gave his consent. The team set out to conquer its rivals in the locality. Soon Jim Shaw, as one of the celebrated Blackburn Rovers, was earning fame, for the team won their matches far and wide. In fact, they covered themselves with glory until each player could hardly find room for the medals, shields and cups that were his share of the triumph.

Young Jim Shaw took his training very seriously. Perhaps it was his Spartan regime that brought on the first signs of fever, but one day, coming back from the woods with a companion, he suddenly decided that the way would seem shorter and the journey made happier if they sang. The singing of Jim Shaw was lusty and enthusiastic. His companion found it amusing at first but after a while began to look at Jim with some anxiety. It seemed that there was something far wrong. He was frightened, especially when Jim refused to be silenced. Leaving him trailing behind, his colleague ran to Jim's house.

'There's something wrong with Jim!' he said breathlessly. 'He will sing, and it's as if he wasn't in his right mind!'

The Shaws stared in astonishment. Jim's singing came to their ears just as they were about to decide that their informant himself was deranged. They ran out and met Jim, who angrily asked them if there was anything wrong with a lad singing to keep his spirits up. A brightness in his eye and a slight flush told the Shaws he wasn't well.

'We'll have the doctor to him,' said William Shaw. 'He's not himself at all. I never knew him behave like this before.'

That Jim had a temperature was apparent from the heat of his brow. That he was much more than fevered the doctor diagnosed in a minute or two with his stethoscope. He shook his head and put away the thermometer.

'If you haven't guessed, I'd better tell you. The lad has pneumonia. You know what that means.'

They knew well enough. It meant linseed and mustard poultices and a battle for the youngster's life. No one had as yet thought that the condition might be treated with drugs. There was nothing more drastic, more brutal in its application than the boiling hot linseed poultice applied to naked flesh.

'Beetles are creatures with their bones on the outside of their bodies, and flesh inside, unlike man, whose bones are on the inside and flesh on the outside . . . ' James rambled.

'Lie still, James,' said his father. 'Forget the beetles.'

The clock ticked the minutes and the hours away. In the kitchen they boiled the linseed in a muslin bag and brought it, dripping from the steaming pot, to lay it on him. He sang again.

> 'Katie Beardie had a cock,
> It sat and crowed upon a rock.
> Wasn't that a dainty cock,
> Said Katie Beardie!'

No one in the family had ever heard the song before. It seemed to come out of Jim's subconscious. Perhaps, they said, he made it up. He stopped singing and moaned, and then cried out for mercy as the boiling linseed came down upon his back. His father held his hand and tried to soothe him, and was relieved when the ordeal was over, at least for a time while the second poultice was prepared. Jim was away in the deep green woods of summer, listening to the birds, smelling the damp air after the rain, looking up at the sky beyond the topmost branches, and vaguely singing his song about Katie Beardie's crowing bird.

'Do you think he will live?' asked Mrs Shaw.

William Shaw didn't know. The doctor had told him never to move Jim from his room but to summon him if there was any change in his breathing. A time came when it seemed that Jim wouldn't be able to get his breath if something wasn't done for him. William Shaw got to his feet and went pounding off for the doctor.

'I am feared for his life, man!' he said.

The doctor knew what it was about. He hurried too, bringing the oxygen he had arranged to have standing by. They lost no time putting the mask to Jim's face. In a moment or two he was over the spasm. The oxygen had staved off death, but there was the crisis to come and that was something William Shaw must wait for. He would know it when it came. There would be a change in Jim's breathing. It might seem that he had stopped breathing altogether. For maybe a minute or two those by his bed-side would think him dead, then, if he had the strength and the will, he would recover and breathe normally, very quietly sinking into a sound sleep. William Shaw dozed and waited, his head jerking forward when he almost fell asleep. Jim went on breathing heavily, painfully, and time meant nothing to either of them. The cock crowed in the shed. Somewhere in the wood an owl cried. The moment came. William Shaw sat and listened and wondered what was different, prepared though he had been for some sign of change. It was hard to tell if Jim was still breathing but he was!

'It's past! It's past, thank God!' William Shaw said

shakily and went through to awaken his wife. 'Sit you by the bed for a while. He's over the crisis now. I must get to my work today. He isn't going to die.'

And Jim no longer rambled about beetles, or sang songs about cockerels. It was a while before he could sip gruel and much longer before his strength was enough to allow him to lift his head without being helped.

'He was well nourished,' said the doctor. 'Never breathed anything but the fresh clean air of the woods. His lungs were as strong as the blacksmith's bellows. We should be thankful for good health, and being able to live in the country. Mind you, it's not the weather for anybody who has been through what the lad has been through. I think he would come on better in a milder place. What about back down on the Ayrshire coast? It's mild down there in the spring and early summer, by all accounts, or you'd never get the early potatoes.'

William Shaw nodded at that. He thought of their long-ago holidays to Craigie on the potato carts. If Jim couldn't go to Craigie there was at least a chance that he might get a place in Ayrshire where Mr Johnstone had considerable influence.

Mr Johnstone was Factor for Skelmorlie Castle estate, at Wemyss Bay. He agreed that the sea air would help to set young Jim on his feet once he was strong enough to get on them. He would have to be well fed. There was a chance that the head woodman at Wemyss Bay would be able to take him.

Jim got on his feet, and Mr Johnstone was as good as his word. He arranged for him to complete his training at Skelmorlie.

4

Axeman

SKELMORLIE CASTLE estate, like many another private estate, was an amenity one. It was cared for and maintained not for the revenue that its timber might produce, as a contribution to estate expenses, but for the attractiveness of its woods and trees. Revenue came from the shooting rights which at that time were rented to the Coates family whose product, the famous Paisley thread, was known to every needlewoman and seamstress in Britain. Skelmorlie's five hundred acres or thereabouts supported a good stock of game. There was a grouse moor. Three keepers tended pheasants and grouse. The woodmen were often recruited as beaters. The rougher land of Skelmorlie, overlooking the road running between Wemyss Bay and Largs, grew some handsome hardwoods which clothed slopes and the banks of dingles running down to the sea. A forester might pause while clearing briar or helping to drive pheasants and see some fine, newly-fitted ship from the Clyde, running its trials on the measured mile a little way out in the Firth. Young Jim Shaw saw what there was to be seen and remembered seeing the sea as he had known it as a small child. The air was good. There was a breath of the sea in it and he knew that it would do him good. It was coming on to high summer. The leaves of oak and ash were out. The thorn was blooming. The gorse had already tarnished. Gulls sailed aloft and old carrion crows and rooks associated with one another on the potato and turnip fields.

It takes time to get used to a new place. Even someone who hasn't suffered an illness like pneumonia finds that his lungs must become accustomed to the change of air. Jim felt sleepy at first and a little short of breath. He ran and found that he became faint because he was asking a little too much of his body all at once. He had come to live in a bothy and he had never lived in one before, but the bothy was a comfortable one. It was snug and not damp. The beds were good. Mrs MacKellar, the wife of the head keeper, knew that the young man had been ill and needed building up. She came in to cook a meal for the two young foresters who occupied the bothy and she was careful to see that Jim Shaw got all the food he needed. Jim's wages had been augmented now that he was away from home. He was earning a pound a week instead of half a crown, but he had to buy his share of food and woodmen are inclined to become very hungry after a hard day out of doors. At the weekends he and his bothy companion would invest in a quarter of a sheep which would be cut up and cooked. They bought their own bread and vegetables from the shop in Upper Skelmorlie and lived like kings on fresh produce which included the early Ayrshire potatoes covered with good farm butter. Mrs MacKellar reported to the factor that he was coming on fine. It was a great responsibility to have a convalescent on her hands. She wanted him to be as fit as a fighting cock. Soon he was, for Mr MacKellar contributed a little variety to the diet, bringing them two or three rabbits a week, an odd hare and once in a while a pheasant, when one met with an unavoidable accident by running under the mower in the hay field.

The young woodmen cultivated another source of supply for now and again boilermakers from the Clyde would sail down on a fishing expedition in some small craft they had made seaworthy and fit for the currents and winds of the Firth. They would ask if they might moor their boat and spend some time at the bothy cooking their meals. Invariably they left fish which the woodmen had for their evening meal or for breakfast. Fish made a welcome change from eggs and bacon or porridge. Jim Shaw's appetite left no doubt that he was recovering fast. Perhaps the only cloud on the horizon was that there seemed little at Skelmorlie that might broaden his experience as a forester, although he might learn something of the control of water supplies.

Skelmorlie estate at this time contained and controlled the water supply of Upper Skelmorlie. The forestry staff were responsible for the filtration plant and the pipe system from the reservoir to the filters from which it was piped to the town. Learning about valves and filters was not particularly exciting but every few weeks Jim would assist at turning off one of the three filtering beds and skimming away the surface grading of fine sand containing impurities piped from the reservoir. The sand itself would be washed and returned to cover graded filtering material through which the reservoir water ran again when valves were reopened. The most interesting aspect of this laborious cleansing was the prospect of recovering golf balls. Skelmorlie reservoir adjoined a golf course and the enthusiastic golfers lost one or two balls almost every time they teed off. The pump-house at the filters was equipped with a sizeable plank into which small nails had been driven in groups of three. This enabled the 'catch' to be set out to dry and then be repainted. A good trade was done with the professional at the golf club and members cheerfully bought back balls they had lost in the reservoir.

That the change seemed to have done his health good Jim reported to his father by letter. That he was in need of another change Jim also made plain.

'There is very little to be learned here, so far as I can see,' he said. 'I think I am not learning enough. What I have learned will slip away from me unless I get back to proper forestry the way it is done at Killearn. I have spoken to Mr Mullins about this. He has mentioned that there is a creosoting plant at Eglington Castle, which he also controls, but I don't know about that. My time is almost up. I think if I could come back and get my reference, maybe I could get somewhere down in England. They say they are crying out for Scotch foresters on the estates down there. . . . '

His father knew exactly what was in Jim's mind. He cautioned him to be patient, to come home and get his reference when he had been examined in the branches of forestry and estate work he had studied.

'There is a place for you here. The old men are getting past it and there should be opportunities with Colonel Blackburn, if you will just hold on and bide your time,' he wrote. 'It doesn't do to be running off to England, when there is so much a good forester can learn here in the north, where forestry has been a much closer study than anywhere else in Britain. Come home. That will do for now.'

Jim read the letter and smiled. He had had six months in the bothy. He had had the fine Ayrshire summer. In the winter there wouldn't be much more to do except duty as a beater at the shoots, a bit of cleaning and clearing in some of the woods, and work at the water filters.

'My time is almost out,' he said to Mr Mullins. 'I think I had better go back and get my reference. I have my tests to take. My father has a place for me and Mr Johnstone approves.'

The Skelmorlie forester nodded and again mentioned the creosoting plant. It wasn't every forester who had experience of timber preservation. At Eglington nothing was wasted. There was a place for him when he wanted it.

At Killearn the tests were duly arranged. Jim Shaw's work in the woods was already evaluated. They knew that he could grow young trees from seed, and transplant seedlings. They knew that he could clean and prune, and lay in and fell a tree, either with the axe alone or with saw, axe and wedges. They only needed to know that he was practical in other ways. That he could make a drain if need be. That he could put up fencing, repair a lead pipe, run 'the electric' to some outbuilding, give an estimate for the building of an outhouse such as a piggery, and answer such questions as the factor, the Carbeth head forester, or the Killearn carpenter and electrician thought to put him.

'You know what you've done. You remember what you've been told. You've no need to worry, lad,' said old Davy Carr. 'They can't ask you anything you can't answer.'

Jim himself was quite confident that he would get his reference. He cut the old lead pipe and sweated in a new section. He remembered about the mixing of mortar and cement. He demonstrated, with the aid of Davy Carr himself, how a floor was laid. When all was over he went home for his tea.

'Well,' said his father. 'At the end of the month you'll know what they think of you.'

William Shaw knew that his son would have no difficulty in convincing the factor that he had acquired a wide knowledge of his trade.

Davy Carr had assured him that he had done well. He told Jim so.

'Never bother your head about it. I know you've pleased them. I took the trouble to have a word with Mr Proctor of Carbeth. He said he didn't expect less from William Shaw's son, and he was well pleased. Mr Johnstone had a smile on his face when they were talking about you. You'll get the money.'

The reward was exactly one shilling a week more than he had been getting at Skelmorlie, a shilling more than an ordinary labourer. At the end of the week he received his sovereign plus one shilling. He was accepted among the qualified. He was a woodman in his own right, earning four shillings a week less than a head forester! He paid half a sovereign towards household expenses, and carried his own axe to the wood with his own sharpening stone.

From now on no one else would use the same axe. When need be he would take time out to hone it with the Shanter stone, a piece of very special stone that came from the River Doon in Ayrshire. It would be his habit to hone his axe before going to fell timber in the morning and perhaps again at midday. He would take a pride in its keen edge. If it needed the grindstone he would report the fact to the foreman or senior forester before going to the toolshed and grinding it, honing it and then finishing it off with his Shanter stone. The Shanter was 'wet' stone and could be used in the wood but the oilstone was only used in the toolshed.

Jim soon acquired skill as an axeman. It would have been odd had he not done so, for Ayrshire axemen were considered the best in Britain at that time. Ayrshire axes had upturned handles. This gave them some slight advantage in delivering a blow to chip away at the base of a large tree in preparation for the saw. 'Laying in' is the tree-feller's secret. When done properly the stump or stool is cut at ground-level, slightly angled so that water will be shed. It will also be a little dished. Making this 'sink' in the stool ensures that if the tree breaks away as it falls, breaking occurs in the base. The trunk itself never shatters or splits. Jim had been well schooled in the axeman's work, of course, but practice makes perfect and apprentices are never given quite the same responsibility as a man who has served his time. He was soon bringing down great trees with the aid of axe and saw. He used the jack and iron wedges, and sometimes the wood demon or chain to strain a tree and prevent a large trunk riding back on the saw, locking it, so that no matter how many men huff, and puff it will not move.

'Never let anyone see you handling the axe carelessly,' said his father. 'Never have it anything but properly honed. A blunt axe isn't just a hopeless tool. It is a sign of an indolent, lazy woodman. Make sure your axe is sharp. Don't have to ask to drop out to stone it, like the day-workers. Don't bash away with it dull like the greedy piece-workers!'

William Shaw was drawing Jim's attention to the fact that on contract felling the casuals employed too often took ten or fifteen minutes going through the motions of sharpening an axe (which was a great deal easier than swinging one) while the piece-workers on the same job were so eager to make money that they hadn't the sense to see that a blunt axe made them toil longer and harder.

The question of axes and their use was raised by the arrival of Jim's elder brother, William, who had been away in America, practising his trade of engineer in Seattle. It had seemed to William that the American two-bitted axe, or double-ended axe, had some advantage over the long-headed axe commonly used by Scottish foresters at that time.

Producing the American axe on his return home William smiled at his father, 'Now don't you think that this will save a woodman sharpening his axe and taking up either his working time, or his dinner-time, doing what only needs to be done once in a day?'

William Shaw regarded the American axe doubtfully.

'Two heads are supposed to be better than one,' he said, 'but if a man sharpens his axe properly and uses it with care, it will be nearly as sharp at the end of the day as at the beginning! The Americans are clever in a lazy way. Prove to me the two-headed axe does something the old axe doesn't, and maybe I'll use one.'

William promised to show how effectively the two-bitted axe did its work. He would lay in a beech for felling! It was a sleety, cold day. William, accompanied by his father and one or two woodmen, stepped off the Killearn drive and took the axe in his hands. He wasn't unfamiliar with the work of an axeman, but he wasn't skilled in the art. As he made his first upward swing the American axe caught on a branch immediately above his head. With more force than was needed, the would-be axeman swept the two-bitted axe backward to cut the small branch. The axe slipped from his grasp, turned neatly in the air and came down with a thud, going right through his foot and splitting his boot. Blood welled up. The demonstration changed from one of axemanship to first aid. They hurried William to the courtyard at Killearn and a pony was quickly harnessed to a gig. On their arrival at his surgery the doctor quickly put five stitches in William's foot.

'Now,' said William Shaw, senior, while his son from America hobbled into the house. 'We'll just put your fancy two-bitted American axes in the shed and let them stay there! If they have any other fancy tools in America they can keep them!'

William Shaw never used the axes from Seattle. His men found a name for them. They called them the two-bitched axes. Their rejection wasn't entirely a testament to conservative outlook. The single-bladed American axe was often used on small timber and operations such as lopping branches from wind-blown trees that had to be cleared before the beetle got to work on the bark. The American rake-toothed crosscut saw, too, found approval among the foresters of the north, particularly at Killearn when William sent his father one of the special saw-setting devices required to keep this kind of crosscut working. The rake-tooth, unlike the 'native' diamond-toothed, or the briar-toothed saws, produced no sawdust but a little ribbon of wood which the teeth that gave the saw its name raked from the cut. Raker or briar, Jim Shaw was content to use whatever he was called upon to use. He was familiar by this time with every kind of tool the forester had and proficient with both the Swedish metal bowsaw and the old wooden bowsaws, kept in tension with a rope twisted by a strip of wood. It wasn't the saw that did the work, he would tell himself, but the hand and the mind behind it, just as it wasn't the axe that brought a seventy- or eighty-foot fir toppling to lie precisely where the feller had decided it must fall. Tree-felling might look a casual

business, but it depended upon the man who could see
where the trees would lie and how they would then be
dragged out without waste of time or damage to adjoining
timber. It gave him a feeling of pride to see his work with
the axe and saw come to the moment when some massive
pine or fir balanced for a moment on the stump and then,
almost as gracefully as it had once swayed in the wind,
came down to the floor of the wood with a swish of
branches that made grass and bracken lie back in the
draught.

'Trees are a long time growing,' he would say to himself. 'They should be brought down with some care and
skill, and not mutilated and murdered by some fool with
an axe.'

He knew himself for a fine axeman, as good as most he
had already encountered, saving, perhaps, his father and
one or two old hands like Davy Carr. While he exulted in
the bringing down of a tree to demonstrate his skill he was
at heart a man who saw more trees growing where trees
had to be felled. The order of his training had been established in the nursery. He was to spend more of his life
planting than felling.

The gale that rocked Craighat wood at this time did
damage everywhere. It shook out the nests of rooks. It
scattered a debris of broken branches and twigs on roads
for miles around. It pushed old, teetering birch tops off
the lower trunks of long-rotten trees. It combed the young
plantations, carried away corrugated iron from farm sheds
and outbuildings, and left its mark far and wide over the
countryside. At Craighat it did what the forester dreads, it
toppled the perimeter trees of a fine plantation and made a
natural channel for itself, felling more and more trees in
layers. This is a weakness of the conifer planting. Roots
never have a deep hold and when the great radial root is
lifted it is as though the carpet has risen. The roots of the
next swaying giant rise too. One tree leans on another.
Soon the front line of the regiment has fallen.

William Shaw didn't need to be told to go to Craighat
wood and see if there was damage. He knew, as he would
have known had he been there in the gale, just where the
blow had taken effect. He called his men the day after the
gale, when there was the usual eerie calm that always
follows such a storm, and told them he wanted them clearing up in Craighat. There would be days of work lopping
branches and releasing one tree trunk from the weight and
tangle of another. Jim, and every other available man,
plodded off to Craighat wood and saw what had happened
on the previous day. They laid their saws on the bank,
took the leather protectors from their smaller axes and
began clearing up the jungle. The fallen trees pleased nobody. There is a great deal of difference between trees
brought down by storm and trees expertly dropped by the
man with the axe. Even climbing under and over the great
mass of branches and broken limbs was tiring enough, but
once the branches had been cut and dragged away there
was more toil, sawing the fallen tree and freeing it from an
upturned root which almost invariably supported the tops
of two or three more. It was both exhausting and dangerous work. The team sawed and cleared and went on
doing so throughout the morning and the afternoon, each
woodman glad of assistance from apprentices and
labourers. Jim watched one of the woodmen working away
on a great trunk which stood across an area of soft, boggy
ground. One end of the tree was elevated by the root to
which it was still attached. The other rested on the root of
a tree not long cut clear. The woodman was preparing to
trim the last of the supporting branches so that the saw
might be used to cut the trunk free when the root that
supported the tip suddenly turned back. It settled in the
earth in which it had once been growing. The tree the
woodman had been trying to clear dropped equally suddenly and the man was all at once lying on his back, held
down by something close to two tons of tree. Its bulk
crushed him deeper and deeper into the soft earth.

William Shaw pounded across the wood and scrambled over trees already cut clear so that he could see what had happened and what could be done. There was no doubt about the gravity of the accident. The victim was pinned down. The tree was a monster. The poor fellow had lost consciousness. His face, drained of blood, looked like that of a corpse. The tree had to be got away from him, and he would have to be rushed to hospital, supposing he survived that long. The axemen rushed to clear a way. The sawyers sawed. Lengths of tree trunk were dragged up to support a lever. The crosscuts had never been pushed and pulled so fast before. Men swarmed everywhere, aware of the urgency. William Shaw was in the middle of it all, giving orders, urging them on.

'He can't live. His back must be smashed!' said one, shaking sweat from his brow and still pulling the crosscut.

That the unfortunate man stood little chance of surviving everyone knew. The soil was soft, but under the weight of such a tree it compacted. A man's backbone was like a tree, soft and pliable when he was a mere sapling, but more rigid when he grew to maturity. The victim of the awful accident was no downy-chinned apprentice, but a grown man.

At length the timber was cut and cleared. The great mass of wood was heaved back and rolled away. A stretcher had been made. Gently, fearfully, the woodmen carried their workmate over the rough ground, down Craighat wood, through the gate, and on to the road where a car was waiting. A doctor had already given the unconscious man an injection but as he climbed into the car along with the head forester he shook his head. This was going to be a one-way journey. Everyone knew it. Glasgow infirmary was a long way away. The injured man would never live long enough to get there. The woodmen went back to the wood and finished their day's work. They thought of all the damage the gale had done. It had almost certainly killed a man, one of their own, a good fellow who had always kept his end up and done his share of whatever rough and hard work there was to be done.

'Well,' they said, as they went home. 'Even if you would like to believe in miracles that kind of miracle can't happen.'

Jim ate his meal in silence, depressed by the awful things that had happened. His stepmother left him to his thoughts until she heard the sound of a car on the road outside.

'Your father's back,' she told him, 'and the way he's talking there it looks as though the poor man isn't dead yet.'

'He's dead,' said Jim. 'Nobody could lie under a weight like that and not have his spine crushed.'

'Ah but he's not dead,' said William Shaw when he came in. 'A miracle, it seems! He had a soft backbone, like the backbone of a weasel, they say. It gave under the weight. Another man would have died on the spot. He's still alive. They say he'll live.'

The woodman didn't die. He survived the ordeal. Although he didn't return to the wood and was bent and crippled, he was able to get about.

Shortly after this near tragedy Jim began to suffer from the same restlessness he had experienced at Skelmorlie. It wasn't that the work at Killearn had changed, but he began, once again, to be concerned about the scope of his experience.

'If I could go to England,' he said more than once, 'or get a recommendation to some place where they do more than is done here!'

'What is done here, you will one day admit,' said his father, 'is the very basis of forestry. This is the finest training ground. The kind of forestry practised here covers it all, hardwood and conifers, nursery work such as you won't find anywhere else. Here we make use of our timber, and plant judiciously.'

Discontent gnaws at a young man, however. He could

see no future except waiting for dead men's shoes. Foresters, although they work hard, live to a ripe old age and
remain active because of the healthy life they have led. It
was no comfort to discover that this or that senior forester
complained of rheumatics and thought he wouldn't be able
to go on much longer. The old men went on, and to tell
the truth, Jim was fond of the old men and would have had
them live for ever.

'I think I'll write to Mr Mullins and ask him about the
creosoting plant at Eglington,' he said one evening.

'Boiling up timber for creosote to soak into it won't
occupy you very long,' William Shaw assured him. 'I
could tell you how it is done, but if you must go you must
go. Kilwinning pleased Burns. Maybe it will please you.'

Shortly afterwards Jim received Mr Mullins's reply.
The job was waiting for him. He could come and start
right away. The only stipulation was that he must live
close to the head forester so that he could be on hand for
his daily instructions. There was a bothy. The conditions
would be as at Skelmorlie, except that he would be paid
the woodman's rate of twenty-one shillings. Jim packed
his things and took himself to Eglington. It was to prove a
disappointment, as he discovered almost the moment he
arrived. The bothy was a ramshackle place, dirty and
damp. The cooking was poor. Things were so unsatisfactory that Jim made a stand and complained. He wanted
to live out, and asked for compensation for the loss of
bothy accommodation. Mr Mullins told him he would
think about it. He didn't come to a decision while Jim
remained at Eglington. The bothy wasn't improved. The
food remained badly cooked from first day until last.

Eglington estate took a pride in making use of whatever
rubbish there was in the way of scrub timber. They used
poplar, birch, willow, any kind of cleared wood, or thinnings, to make fence posts, gates, props etc., holding that
creosote made useless timber as durable as oak or larch. A
good amount of this kind of material, cut in the Eglington

woods, went to maintain Bogside Racecourse, where fences
and jumps, rails etc. had to be kept in repair. This would
have been false economy in general estate maintenance but
young woodmen, even those out of their apprenticeship,
learn to keep their opinions to themselves! The creosoted
poplar and willow may not have rotted in the ground quite
so quickly as they would have done had they been used
without the treatment, but they proved resilient when it
came to nailing and stapling. Fences took on a drunken
appearance and looked very untidy even when they weren't
used as rubbing posts by cattle and sheep.

Jim knew his mistake. He was full of remorse at not
having listened to his father. He wondered what would be
said when he wrote home and told him that he couldn't
stand Eglington any more than Skelmorlie. The letter
remained unwritten. He pondered over his problem for
several days until he met a friend, Robin Boyd, who with
his brother worked at Eglington but wanted away.

'What's wrong with you, Jim?' he asked.

'I'm getting nowhere. I wish I had never come. I would
rather do anything than stay here, but I don't know what
to say to my father.'

'You're like me,' said Robin. 'I'm getting nowhere. I
want to get out. I want a job where I can get time to study.
I want to be an accountant. I'm going up to Glasgow to
see about getting on the Police Force. An eight-hour day
it is there! You can study all the rest of the time. You can
go to evening classes and be what you like.'

'Or be a policeman,' said Jim. 'I had an uncle who was
in the Partick Division, a detective sergeant, he was.'

Or be a policeman. The truth was he didn't see himself
as a policeman either, but there would be time to study and
there were good libraries and evening classes in Glasgow.

'Do you think I might come up with you?' he asked.

Robin Boyd gave him a friendly thump on the shoulder.
'You come with me. We'll take the plunge together. We'll
give Mr Mullins our notice on the same day. We'll go to

Glasgow and fill up the form and maybe we'll be on the same beat.'

Jim still didn't know how he was going to break the news to his father. Joining the police was a drastic step. It wasn't making use of his training. He had always said that what was wrong was he would forget what he had been taught.

'I'm with you,' he said.

That afternoon they waited for Mr Mullins and told him that they intended to join the Glasgow Police. Mr Mullins shrugged his shoulders. He really didn't care what they did. He would find a couple of woodmen who would be content with the creosoting plant and the not too strenuous work of keeping the racecourse in trim.

'As you please,' he said.

They went their ways, each to gather his clothes and personal things in preparation for the visit to Glasgow Central Police Station, where they would, in due course, fill up the form and be sent for a medical examination. Jim remembered his bout of pneumonia and knew it hadn't left a weakness. He was sure he could pass any test the Police might set.

5

Guardsman Shaw

At Glasgow Central Division that August morning in
1913, the officer receiving the would-be recruits took Jim
Shaw's application form and checked it over. It gave his
occupation, the names of both parents, references that included Mr Johnstone, Factor to Doonholm in Ayrshire
and Killearn, Stirlingshire, as well as Colonel Blackburn
and the minister at Killearn. The sturdy young woodman
was just the sort of youngster they were looking for, a lad
who could look after himself and cope with trouble at
Glasgow Cross on a Saturday night, when the city was
owned by every bandy-legged little fighting cock with a
bottle in his hand.

'You won't be in the parks and among the trees very
often, Shaw,' he said, 'and I doubt whether you'll be
allowed to carry an axe in the Gallowgate, but if you can
pass the doctor and do your sums this afternoon, you're the
sort we're recruiting.'

Jim Shaw smiled to himself. He wasn't too much concerned about carrying an axe, or too excited about a beat
in the Gallowgate. He was hopeful about enrolling for
evening classes, getting down to some study which might
fit him for better things—botany, estate management . . .
The arithmetic didn't trouble him at all. He had been well
schooled. He could work out the cubic capacity of tree

trunks of different diameters as fast as a bookmaker cal-
culating the odds. He finished his sums, answered the
geography questions, and picked up the paper which was
to test his ability to write English—an essay. The subject,
'Why I want to be a policeman!' There it was. He scratched
his head for a moment and smiled to himself again. What
would they say if he wrote, 'I want to be a policeman so
that I can get enough free time to study estate management and botany. When I have studied these subjects and
passed examinations in them I hope to apply for a position
as a forester in England. I shall, of course, discharge my
duty as a policeman to the very best of my ability at all
times. I trust that the Police Authority will keep me
working the right shift so that I can pursue my studies.' He
had a feeling that although he had been told he was just
the kind of young fellow they were looking for, he might
find himself turned down if he wrote what was in his mind!
Picking up the pen he began, 'I want to be a policeman
because I have always admired the way a police officer
exerts his authority in moments of emergency or crisis. I
understand that it is essential for the good order of society
that the law be upheld and the confidence of the public in
the justness of the law be maintained . . . ' It was a wordy
essay because he felt the need to cover his real motive for
joining the police. He was relieved when it was done and
he had handed it in. Soon after he was told that he had been
accepted. His character references had been checked. His
arithmetic marked. His essay approved. He would be paid
twenty-nine shillings a week, provided with a Glasgow
City Police helmet, tunic, trousers, three-quarter coat,
greatcoat, cape and baton. He would buy his own boots,
however. The police had never admitted that a policeman
needed boots! They made no allowance for them. During
the next six weeks, Police Constable James Shaw, No. A
56, would parade for instruction and drill at the Muster
Hall at nine o'clock precisely. It would be an eight-hour
day. When it ended he could go back to his lodgings in

the house of P.C. Sinclair and study for all he was worth
—the police manual, hackney carriage regulations,
licensing laws, and a score of city by-laws he had never
dreamed existed! There would be time for botany later,
he told himself sorrowfully. Soon he might be able to
attend lectures at the Botanical Gardens and the Technical
Institute in St George's Square.

What dreams Jim Shaw might have had were banished
from his mind by lectures at the Muster Hall where
Inspector Simcox and P.C. MacDonald talked, not of
crenate and dentate leaves and branches with alternate
leaves, but of the way to handle a Glasgow Cross drunk
with an inborn resentment of all policemen, and how to
avoid being brought down by a swinging bottle! They explained about tact and politeness. They drew attention to
the wisdom of backing to a brick wall and not to a shop
window, through which one might be pushed. They talked
of a different sort of bird from those Jim Shaw had ob-
served in the forest. They told him of the gin-happy ladies
of the pavements and the close-mouths, women whose
vocabularies were extensive and whose language was as
incomprehensible to a stranger to Glasgow as Gaelic to the
Sassenach. Jim Shaw took note of what he was told. He
stepped smartly when mustered for foot drill. He went
home to his lodgings knowing his brightest dreams were
fading away. After six weeks he would be on the beat doing
eight hours, odd-numbered constables on early shift, even
numbered on late shift, alternating every six weeks. What
course could he study at the Technical Institute when for
six weeks he wouldn't be free for lectures? He pondered
upon this when he went home to break the news to William
Shaw that he was no longer following the calling for which
he had been trained, but soon to be walking the pavements
of the Gallowgate.

William Shaw shrugged his shoulders. 'Policeman?
Well, you can believe me, you will be back to your trees
yet! The police won't do for you, my lad. If things had

turned out a wee bit different you might have been away to Willie McIlwraith at Burnham Beeches, down in England. Willie could have taken you on there.'

Jim nodded ruefully. He hardly needed to be told that he was restless, and as impetuous as any youngster of his age, but at the same time he was conscious that even at Killearn things weren't quite what they had been. The old men were going. The estate was employing more casual and untrained labour in the forest. Elsewhere it was even worse. Few estates were spending money on their woods. Many were taking out without putting anything in and a policy of reaping without sowing could only lead to famine.

When he went back again to Glasgow he was homesick. He longed for the soft green woods of Killearn and the fresh air of the open country. Instead of these he walked the beat for the first time in the company of an old policeman. He discovered the sour odour of the public house when its doors and cellar flaps were opened in the morning. He became used to the taste of chimney fires in the damp air when some tenement housewife stuffed a lighted newspaper up the flue and set the soot burning.

'At Killearn they will be burning bark peelings,' he told his companion, 'and the deer will be slipping through the woods like brown shadows. I wish I could be at home!'

The old policeman shrugged his shoulders. 'It's the same for every recruit. Glasgow is full of recruits who moon about, feeling sick for Skye or Strathspey. You either get over it, or you go back to where you came from.'

Jim plodded down the street and wondered how he was going to get over it, when he couldn't take a proper course and couldn't study in his lodgings for the noise of P.C. Sinclair's three young children.

The problem of the children was solved, however. A room became vacant in the Police Barracks and he moved in at the end of his initial training. He went out and bought himself one or two books. He attended what lectures he could at the Botanical Gardens and the Institute, but he couldn't enrol for either of the subjects he wanted to study. Added to this difficulty was the awful temptation of the barracks recreation room, where there was a billiards table, and more company than the young forester had ever enjoyed at home or at Skelmorlie.

His first turn of duty on his own beat was on day shift. He was careful to scrutinise the hackney carriage plates to see that they were clean and readable, and to see that no carter left his nags too long feeding on oats while he dallied in the public house supping ale. He gently intervened when aggressive women sought to tear one another's hair out. He turned a deaf ear to muttered curses against the 'bloody poliss'. On Saturday night he kicked the broken glass from the pavement into the gutter and hoped he wouldn't have to use his baton on any tenement Davids who saw his broad frame in the image of Goliath. His companions in the Barracks exchanged information and asked about wild characters who travelled from one beat to another. In due course he took in the drunk and disorderlies, careful to avoid the simple but hard to establish charge of being drunk or under the influence. He had been warned of the folly of arresting a man for breaking glass on the pavement when bottles fell like coconuts from the tree and what goes up usually comes down. Nothing that happened taxed his nerve or troubled him very much until he was summoned urgently to help arrest a German Reservist, set upon returning to the land of his infant nurture—without paying his landlady her due.

'This one isn't going to come, Shaw,' said the older constable. 'I can't manage him by myself. He's wild. He refuses to listen. The landlady has his bag and she won't part with it unless he pays her. I don't blame her. He's a pig-headed German and thinks he can do as he likes!'

Jim felt tightness in his stomach. It was bound to come sooner or later, a situation where tact and reason didn't work and violence was inevitable.

'I never met a German,' he said, 'but from what the

papers say about them, they're an arrogant, aggressive lot. How will we set about him?'

'We'll act as one,' said his companion. 'We'll go in together and the minute you are in, get behind a chair or a table, lift it, and drive him to the wall! That way we'll pin him and get the better of him before he can do us any damage.'

They went up into the tenement together, aware of the neighbours watching them from the well of the stairs.

'Right then!' said the older constable. 'Both together.'

The German turned to attack them, his face contorted with anger. Jim stepped neatly behind a chair. His companion did likewise. Blows that might have laid one of them low fell on air. They battled with the chairs against an adversary whom one or both of them might soon be destined to meet again. The chairs clashed and clattered for a minute or two until the German found himself held against the wall. He cursed with a vehemence that made Jim Shaw laugh with relief but the arrest was made. A company of ragged children followed them down the street to Central Division calling names.

'Dirty German!' they shouted. In less than six months the cry would be louder and draw a much larger audience. Jim Shaw was glad when at last they bundled the prisoner into the cells and someone was summoned to explain to him exactly what the law was, and what would happen to him now.

'Them Germans want to run the world their way!' said the sergeant in charge. 'They are sending for their Reservists, it seems. Well, I'm on the Reserve myself! When they send for me I'll pay my bill.'

Jim was on night shift when news of war came. He was patrolling his beat near Queen Street Station and West Nile Street when he heard the newsboys calling the morning headline, 'War Declared! War Declared!' He went off duty at a great pace, wondering what would happen now. The barracks in Clyde Street was a hubbub of conversation. Police reservists were gathering their things together and leaving to report.

'Lad, it won't be long before we're all away,' said an old hand. 'They'll have nobody on the beat in Glasgow at all. You won't find me at the Cross on a Saturday night for all the money in the world. I'm for putting a stop to the Kaiser before it's too late. You wait and you won't be there before it's over!'

The following day the beats were extended because the police were undermanned. Jim Shaw plodded the street and knew that he couldn't wait much longer. As soon as he could, he would volunteer. Exactly a month later, he came off duty and found the barracks recreation room deserted.

'Where are the lads?' he asked a man coming out.

'Gone to enlist. The whole lot of them.'

The news dismayed him. They might have let him know! He turned about and ran for all he was worth back to the Cross and the recruiting office. A cheer greeted him as he joined the queue.

'You nearly got left behind, Jim!'

He laughed. 'What lot are we joining?'

'What else but the Guards?'

'Very well then,' he said, 'the Scots Guards'. It seemed as though the entire Glasgow Police Force was there, hundreds of policemen, from new recruits just finished their probationary period to old hands with years of service behind them.

'Hurry up!' they joked. 'Don't keep us standing here, like the unemployed, until the war is over.'

Slowly the queue fed into the recruiting office. Jim signed his name. J. Shaw, Police Constable No A. 56. He received a travel warrant for Caterham. It was dated just far enough ahead for him to go back to Killearn and break the news to his father, leaving his things at home and going south on a special train, along with policemen from Dundee, Edinburgh, Aberdeen and Perth, all of them destined for the Guards. All they took with them was their shaving kit and a towel. Relatives who came to see them off in Glasgow gave them whisky to drink to celebrate their enlistment. They took the gifts and sat all the way talking excitedly about the war and what they would do to the Kaiser's Army. The whisky was ignored until they reached London.

At Euston they looked with dismay at the gift bottles. They could never drink the stuff now and most of them were teetotallers.

'We can't just leave it here,' said one. 'Could we not give it away to some of these poor porters on the platform?'

The solution seemed a perfect one.

'Have a drink with us!' they called. The porters reached out eagerly for the whisky bottles. Soon they were well away, lolling about or sitting befuddled on their trolleys, blessing the generous Scots policemen.

'And may you chase old Kaiser Wilhelm right back to Berlin!' they shouted.

Jim Shaw grinned back at them. The world seemed to have changed completely in a month. The station was peopled with men in khaki and crowded with civilians coming off trains, although he could hardly believe they were all destined for Caterham. They left Euston in a crowd and stood in the street, hesitating over which way to go. At the Tower Scots Guards reservists were on duty. It would be a great thing to call there and say hello, but how to get there? Ask a policeman? They climbed aboard a bus and sat down, offering their money and receiving tickets, their Scots accent and their Doric phrases making what they said unintelligible to the poor conductor. The bus sailed on, threading its way through horse-drawn brewers' drays and cabs and coster barrows. It was all very different from Glasgow Cross and they had gone more miles than their tickets permitted when the conductor decided they must get off.

'Wrong way,' he said, shaking his head and jerking his thumb.

The policemen clattered off the bus and stood looking back towards the city. Ask a policeman? London was supposed to be well stocked with Highlandmen serving in the police force, but they too had probably gone off to join the Guards or the Black Watch. It was hard to make out what these Cockney boys were talking about! They crossed the road and waited for a bus going in the opposite direction, examining their warrants and travelling instructions while they waited.

'If the bus hurries maybe we'll be in time for the train to Caterham!' said Jumbo Goodbrand; 'but the Tower will have to wait for another day. This time it's London Bridge we want. They'll have us on the carpet if we report late!'

The very thought of reporting late at the depot made them rush on to the bus when it came. They reached London Bridge and entrained for Caterham with barely enough time to spare. The journey down to Surrey had them speculating again. It was clear that they weren't the only recruits joining the Guards.

'Now,' said Jumbo when they reached Caterham. 'I'm told it's a mile and a half, and it's uphill and we're not a rabble. So if you'll just agree to take my command for a mile and a half, we'll march there in column of four. They'll see we have some discipline and self-respect. We can't go streaming up the road like a Rothesay outing coming off the quay!'

It took a few minutes for the crowd to thin out. The policemen stayed together. Jumbo called for a marker and they fell in, turned on their marker, and marched off, swinging their arms unselfconsciously because they were used to public appearances. At the depot entrance an orderly sergeant stepped forward to see them march in. His cane was tucked under his elbow. His moustache bristled as he gazed at them from beneath the visor of his cap. They looked to their front, and waited for Jumbo's command. Jumbo saw the orderly officer standing a few paces behind the sergeant and marched on for as many paces as his squad of sixty-four needed to clear the entrance. 'Squad!' he barked. 'Squad, halt!' They stood to attention. The orderly sergeant's grim expression didn't change. He took over at once. Jumbo looked him in the eye with satisfaction. They marched forward as smartly as ever, across the asphalt, on to the grass, right on until they seemed to be going to collide with a tree. The orderly sergeant brought them to a halt and allowed them to fall out.

'You stay here until accommodation is found for you. Rations will be issued at seven o'clock. You keep it up and stick together. I think we might make a squad of you.'

He turned smartly on his heel and marched away across the grass, leaving them with the impression that although civilians might sometimes flop on the ground and loosen their collars, he never did. The scene about them wasn't at all what they had expected. Men were sitting on the grass everywhere, talking, smoking, waiting. Some were stretched out with their hands behind their heads. It was like a police picnic without the women folk, only much more congested. Jim Shaw stared up into the branches of the tree. It was an oak with a fine crop of acorns coming. He little thought that he would have to sleep under that tree until the following day and then, after much moving around, they would be admitted to the mobilisation sheds. They would wear the 'uniform' in which they had arrived for almost six weeks. It would be four weeks before they were issued with a rifle. The British Army wasn't going to rush at the Germans and try to drive them back with raw recruits. Jim wondered when they would get to France. The war might be over before they got there!

The squad of sixty-four was taken over by a drill sergeant who relaxed sufficiently to tell them that they had a head start on other recruits because of their drill training in the police. He would make them march with a precision they had never dreamed of in Glasgow, and turn them into an automatic squad, capable of drilling without

command beyond the first order, counting in their heads
as they went through the drill paces. They began to appreciate the nature of personal discipline. The newspapers
might talk about Prussians but the Guards would stand
firm, no matter if the heavens fell and the earth opened!

The squad drilled hour after hour, and day after day.
Roving drill sergeants seemed to march down upon them
the moment their own sergeant allowed them to fall out,
and they were back on the marker, measuring their paces,
pulling their chins in, looking to their front, wheeling,
turning about, marching, counter-marching. In the intervals between the staccato commands of their instructor
they would hear the commands of drill sergeants marching
squads all around them. They had long since given up
asking themselves if they would march against the Germans and stamp them into the ground instead of shooting
them but four drills every day produced a smartness that
surprised even their instructor. Soon their precision was
being commented upon by their officers. Major-General
Sir Francis Lloyd came to inspect them as they drilled
without command, and promised them a post of honour
before they went to France. They would be the guard at
the opening of the first War Parliament in November.
After that they might consider themselves ready for the
front and join their battalion in France.

They went to France in December, but not as a squad.
The battalion needed replacements in different companies.
Jim and two companions went to the reserve line behind
the 1st Battalion at Quinchy, between La Bassée and
Béthune. They weren't to meet the German attack until
the débâcle at the brickfields when the 1st Battalion was
mined and blown to oblivion, losing between 500 and 600
men. It was the day the German Army promised to give
Kaiser Wilhelm a present of the Channel ports on his
birthday, January 25th, 1915.

It seemed to Jim Shaw that the Germans had drilled
almost as steadily as the Guards themselves. They came in

blocks of sixteen abreast and sixteen deep, and although
they toppled like trees being axed, they came on through
the smoke and dust and thunder of the guns that pounded
the brickworks. What had hitherto been somewhat remote and distant was all at once there, bullets, grenades,
shell-burst and the flowers of the forest, as the old song
said, all weeded away.

Ahead of them Jim Shaw and his companion, Jack
Lamb, could see a solitary British gun being served by
seemingly tireless artillerymen. The gun was continually
under small arms and heavier fire and it was inevitable that
it would be knocked out. When it ceased firing, the sole
survivor of the gun team, a fair haired, tall young artillery
officer, came to beg two guardsmen to assist him in serving
the gun. Guardsmen they might have been, with little or
no knowledge of shells or gun drill, but Shaw and Lamb
stepped forward and took the place of the dead gunners.
They were shown how to unscrew the noses of the shells to
make them more lethal at close range and the gun began
its deadly work once more. The guardsmen grinned
through the smoke and wiped grime from their faces each
time the gun recoiled and settled in the mud again. They
saw the name chalked on its barrel—Doctor Morgan.
'Good old Doctor Morgan!' they cheered. The enemy
didn't cheer. They didn't care for Doctor Morgan's medi-
cine. The guardsmen shook hands with each other and
with the lieutenant who had named the gun after his father.
It was a long time before the messages and signals passed
back from the La Bassée brickfield reached the artillerymen's headquarters and relief came, but in time it came
and the guardsmen stood down. The Kaiser was being
denied his birthday present at a fearful cost. The Scots
shed no tears over that, but they grieved for their dead
comrades.

There were to be other battles for Guardsman Shaw and
Guardsman Lamb. Jim Shaw fought on, at Festubert, at
Neuve Chapelle and Loos. Between spells in the line he

thought of home and the woods of Killearn and Ayrshire, wondering if he would ever see them again, or would lie with thousands more, in the mud. There were men who claimed to have heard the nightingales singing when there was a lull in the night's barrage. Jim had never heard the nightingale at Killearn and probably wouldn't have known the bird's song had he heard it. Night was often as bright as day and men buried their heads and waited to see if death would come to them or a neighbour. At Loos the stitching of the machine gun did more than throw up spurts of earth on the mounds the Guards were crossing. It found Jim Shaw, and he took bullets in both arms and in his heel. He knew the cloying warmth of his own blood and began to crawl back. He was in good company. There were others crawling because the stretcher bearers were too occupied to come and carry them out, or had themselves fallen. As he crawled the one-time axeman wondered if he would ever be able to work in the woods again.

They took him back to England, to Ipswich and the hospitals through which the wounded and the maimed passed for treatment and rehabilitation. Jack Lamb was there too, along with many more. They went for massage and electrical treatment. They marked time among the crippled and took tea with charitable ladies who could not do enough for them. They told their stories but spared the ladies the details of such events as the Kaiser's birthday. On one of their outings they were received with great enthusiasm by a young woman who sought no more excuse than the Scots Guards' insignia. Her brother, she said, a lieutenant in the artillery, had written to tell her of the bravery of the guardsmen who had stood with him in La Bassée. 'Good old Doctor Morgan!' they exclaimed. By an extraordinary coincidence they found themselves talking of Doctor Morgan to the sister of their sometime lieutenant. Soon they were off to meet Doctor Morgan himself! The world had become small again.

It was to be a long time before what had begun with the

Kaiser's birthday ended for Jim Shaw. He marched and counter-marched again, although he wasn't fit for France. They posted him to the Military Police after he had been a while with his old battalion. They had him schooled in maintaining good order and discipline among a variety of troops, some of whom were reluctant to do what was required of them without punishment. While he soldiered on Jim wondered about the world and what it would be like for those who survived the war.

'When it's over what will you do?' people would ask one another.

The pessimists doubted that it would ever end, or that they would live to see it, even in hospital blue.

'When it's over,' Jim Shaw would say, 'I hope I can get back to planting some trees and clearing up the mess they've made of the woods all over the country.'

His father had told him what was happening. Acres upon acres of woodland had gone down to feed the war machine. Timber that might have served two generations had been sacrificed. The devastation was to be seen everywhere. Hills that had once been topped by plantings, clothed in fine hanging woods of oak and beech and ash, were now bare and ugly, like the back of some pest-infested animal. The young trees hadn't been thinned. They had been cut down, extracted by men who cared little for timber or the state in which they left the wood when they dragged the spoils away, but then the same ruthlessness was being applied everywhere. Horses, for instance, were being commandeered to haul wagons and gun limbers, no matter what their condition, or what their value as stock or stud animals. The world valued nothing. Life was cheap and dealers were there to exploit everything exploitable. The merchants had a keener ear for a profit than the rumble of gunfire.

Jim Shaw was among the optimists. A man who believes in growing an oak or a beech is dedicated to optimism. He looked at what books he could gather together and planned to take the first opportunity to get back to his calling as soon as the war was ended. He would walk in the country in his off-duty periods and study the growth of the tree in the hedge, see how the seedling tried to climb above the thorns and how the untended hedges grew and flourished when no one had the time to cut them back. He looked at the oak gall and the bark beetle. He pondered on the ways of birds with insects and caterpillars, and worked out how he would plant a particular stretch of the Downs, if any-one gave him the opportunity to do so! He longed to go back and plant the slopes of Killearn and work alongside men like Davy Carr.

'It won't go on for ever,' he said. 'It can't go on. There will be nothing left if this waste continues, and war is nothing but waste, waste of our resources either in men or in timber!'

He wasn't the only invalided soldier to say so, but the end of the war wasn't to come for many months. The rape of the woods was going ahead at a pace that rivalled the loss of life in France. Every day in the forests of southern England hundreds and hundreds of fine trees toppled and were as quickly cleared of their branches to go for wagon-making, for jetty-building, for making railway sleepers, for shipbuilding, for pitprops and a thousand other most urgent uses. Jim Shaw was again thinking of the future, but a romantic future. He was planning to get married. He was being optimistic. The young lady of his choice knew nothing about the forest, or a forester's life. She had hardly been outside of the city for she worked and lived in London, where she was a supervisor with the telephone service.

6

Pitprops and Portuguese

M iss Edith Alice Hutchins was an exceptional woman. She might have seen very little of the country beyond London and the home counties but she convinced Jim Shaw, if he needed convincing, that he must get back to the forest. Why he had ever left it to go to the police she would never understand! When the war was over and they were free to do as they pleased they would have no more to do with the city if they could help it. The woods were so peaceful and beautiful, she said. In the spring of 1918 they seemed particularly so. Miss Hutchins heard the banns read at St Margaret's Church at Lee, which is near Blackheath. On March 30th they were married and with ten days' leave Jim Shaw took his bride off north to Stirlingshire. There she saw the beauty that was Loch Lomond, the Campsie Fells and the woods of Killearn. They would live in the country, Jim promised her. They would walk in the woods again. The war might go on a while yet. There was no sign of victory in the news from France. Instead the papers carried their usual long lists of casualties, among the names many that Jim Shaw recognised, boys from the Killearn school, lads who had worked for the railway, for Killearn estate, postmen, gamekeepers, farmers. He carefully and sorrowfully cut items from the news columns and stuffed them in his wallet. Brave men and bravery were commonplace enough now. The long-dead beckoned fresh legions that hurried to join them. The war widows went off to work in munitions factories and only the disabled were excused when the call was for every man who could hold a rifle. Kitchener was drowned but his finger still pointed from posters on hoardings.

Jim Shaw would have gone again, but they asked no more of him in the line of battle. He was already classified C3, a disability which he couldn't deny. It not only made him inadequate as a rifleman. It spoiled his one-time skill at golf. The honeymoon was short. Jim returned to Hastings. His wife went back to the London telephone service desk. She would get down to see him when she could. They saw no particular hardship in parting when thousands of husbands and wives couldn't hope to see one another at all.

There was no posting for which Jim could apply in order to set up house or rent rooms. He had to be satisfied with things as they were until an item on the company notice board caught his attention. He stood and considered it for quite a while. It seemed to apply to his own case and background.

'Anyone with experience of timber and wood, extraction of trees, etc. should apply to the undersigned at Company Headquarters.' It was headed, Woodmen, Sawmill Men, Timber Workers. Jim rubbed his chin and thought hard. In the meantime someone peered over his shoulder and warned him about the way the army ensnared its 'volunteers', getting musicians to move pianos and 'men with a knowledge of timber' to carry railway sleepers!

'Just the same,' he said, 'I think I'll go along and see the adjutant. You never know, and it would be better than drilling chaps with clumsy feet who don't know whether they're coming or going.'

He knocked on the adjutant's door, waited to be summoned, stepped in, came to attention, saluted and gave his rank and name.

'Shaw, sir,' he said, 'James Lymburn Shaw. My trade or profession, sir, woodman.'

The adjutant called for records. 'Policeman,' he said. 'Glasgow, enlisted 1914 . . . Woodman?'

'I am a woodman, sir. My father is head woodman to Colonel Blackburn of Killearn, Stirlingshire. I was in the police for a year because I had hoped to further my education in Glasgow, sir. It didn't work out. I couldn't enrol for a course. The police kept me at it on late and early shifts.'

'Unfortunate, Shaw,' said the adjutant. 'Now you want to leave us and get back to the woods, eh? Well, if you have the experience, good luck to you. Your record is good. No one can say you haven't done your best.'

He passed over a slip of paper.

'Write to this gentleman giving details of your qualifications. If they think you're suitable they'll send for you for an interview. Just be sure you tell the whole truth and nothing but the truth. A lot of men try for things they don't know the first thing about!'

'If it's forestry I don't need to worry,' Jim Shaw told himself as he went off to write to James Calder, Timber Controller, Ministry of Supply, Dean Street, London.

'My father is head forester at Killearn,' he wrote. 'I was trained there, and at Skelmorlie. I can forward references to substantiate this. I passed tests in estate work, building, plumbing, estimating, etc. I have felled timber with axe and saw. I have extracted timber from woodlands. I know how to handle horses and men. I have considerable experience of nursery work and tree-planting. I was for a year in the Glasgow Police, which I joined in the hope of being able to pursue the study of botany and estate management. I can give the following names as reference. . . ' The letter was written with great care. His old schoolmaster would have approved of it and given him full marks. A week or two passed before he had a reply: 'You will report to Mr James Calder at Dean Street for interview regarding the above, and bring copies of references or testimonials you may have for inspection.' He could hardly wait to get up to London.

Mr James Calder knew Mr MacGowan, timber merchant, who dealt with William Shaw of Killearn. He undoubtedly knew William Shaw, although he didn't say so. Jim Shaw relaxed after the first minute or two and talked about his training.

'I hope to get back to forestry when the war is over, sir,' he said, 'and if there is work I could do that would be more important than drilling men or keeping good order and discipline, and it had to do with woods, I would be glad to be directed to it.'

'You most certainly will be directed to it, Shaw,' said James Calder, 'and if you can get work out of the Portuguese who are supposed to be producing pitprops for the South Wales mines, you could make a name for yourself! I'm told it is almost impossible to get them to do what is wanted. They are the most awkward fellows that were ever formed into a Labour Corps. We just aren't getting the pitprops away. You can't make steel, coal a ship, run a train, unless you get coal. You can't mine without pitprops. It's a simple matter up to there. After that you meet this problem of the mutinous, lazy foreigners.'

Jim Shaw was to discover that the poor Portuguese were very much maligned but that was some considerable time later.

'I'll do my best to get pitprops,' he promised. 'How many men are there and where do I go?'

'The place is Presteigne in Radnorshire. You'll take charge of 150 men, two of whom will act as interpreters. The remainder haven't a word of English. You will be responsible to the Divisional Officer at Cirencester, Professor H. A. Pritchard, and you will go down there without delay. I expect results, but I warn you this won't be easy and Presteigne is not a soft number for draftees from the army!'

Presteigne came to Jim Shaw, it seemed, after he had sat for interminable hours in a railway carriage. He got out, feeling stiff and weary, and gazed upon the great mounds of timber that littered the railway yard.

'They've been cutting trees here at a fine pace,' he said to the railway porter.

The porter shrugged his shoulders. 'They've been piling it in, but they tell me they've more than a hundred times this lot lying in the woods and some of it no use for anything. That lot is supposed to be ash.'

Jim didn't need to be told what it really was. His experienced eye had already classified the timber he could see. There was no ash, but great stacks of sweet chestnut and beech. Chestnut might have been all very well in small diameter for splitting and making picket fences. The beech would make furniture, but he guessed that the Ministry had commandeered ash for wagon and lorry frames. Neither beech nor sweet chestnut would serve this purpose.

'So what will happen to this lot?' he mused aloud.

A little man in uniform standing a few feet away came and answered his question.

'What will happen? They'll fill up more forms. Commandeer more trees! The merchants will have a field day, and then, when the ash comes they'll lose it under the pitprops they are supposed to be loading in the wagons for the mines. That stuffed shirt of a Major Cobbett will be down here, cursing everybody and whacking his breeches with his cane. Wait until you meet Major Cobbett.'

'I've met a few terrors in my time,' said Jim Shaw quietly. 'I've met the drill sergeants at Caterham and the Germans at Loos and La Bassée. I'm not likely to get frightened now. I can't imagine how anybody accepted sweet chestnut and beech for ash!'

'You'll understand when you meet the boys who run the game! Just you wait! Yesterday he was here, whacking his leg and bullying everybody. "Major Cobbett," I said, "you may be the top man in the army, but here I am captain of the railway and I give the orders! If you don't accept that, I'll have one of my porters throw you out of the railway yard." He didn't care for that, I can tell you.'

Jim Shaw went off to find accommodation which had been arranged for him at the Temperance Hotel, where Mrs Millichamp, the manageress, welcomed him. He was in civilian clothes again. The 'timber' officers advertised their position by wearing British warms and visored caps. That at least one of them, Major Cobbett, carried a cane, Jim Shaw was soon to find out. He was busy trying to see what timber there was that was any use when he was harshly hailed by a gentleman who prodded him in the back. Not even the drill sergeants of Caterham addressed a man as 'Hey you!' and stuck a cane in his back. Jim Shaw had the hasty temper of his race. He turned round, whipped the cane out of its owner's grasp and quickly snapped it in two before handing him the pieces.

'You were wanting to say something to me? he asked quietly.

The overweight gentleman in the British warm was lost for words. It was quite some minutes before he recovered. By that time, assuming that the major really had nothing beyond four-letter words, Jim Shaw was away about his business. The railway staff looked on. The sometime guardsman didn't look the sort of man anyone was going to push very hard without getting pushed back. Had they seen the motto of the Scots Guards, and known a word or two of Latin, they would have understood completely.

'I'm told that the Portuguese give a lot of trouble,' Jim Shaw remarked to the stationmaster in the morning.

'They complain,' said the stationmaster, 'but nobody understands them, and nobody tries. Maybe you have a word or two of their language?'

Jim grinned. He had been in charge of a squad of Portuguese for a time, trying to teach them the rudiments of British foot-drill and commands. His companion in this enterprise had been a Welshman who had likewise been supplied with Portuguese translations of the British order of foot-drill. Try as he might Jim could never get his orders across, while his Welsh counterpart seemed to manage. 'I speak in Welsh,' he told him. 'They don't understand it any more than they understand English, but somehow they do what I want. Maybe they don't like the English!' Maybe the Portuguese here resented the English, but Jim had a suspicion that they hated the portly gentleman in the British warm who treated them like cattle and ignored their wants. Two interpreters came to him, voluble fellows called Gomez and da Silva. They quickly explained the unhappiness of their compatriots. Nothing was right. There would be no production until the Portuguese were happy. Tomorrow perhaps, before he began giving orders, Meester Shaw would meet a deputation and convey his wishes to the men while they conveyed their grievances to him.

The following morning Jim Shaw looked at his Portuguese Labour Corps. They were swarthy. They scowled. They appeared more dangerous, in their berets and blouses, than he had expected. They gazed at him from beneath dark brows. He noted the flash of their eyes and the whiteness of their teeth when they spat out their angry words.

'What do they say, Mr Gomez, Mr da Silva?' he asked.

The interpreters spoke in their own language and there was silence.

'Food, tools, bullying, slow ways, stupid men who don't know anything about work and have never done any in their lives, ignorant men like the fat major!'

Jim had hardly a chance to hear the interpreter before the mustered Portuguese began to talk again. He held up his hand for silence.

'I will hear a deputation of six,' he said. 'The rest will go and do whatever they were doing.'

The deputation began to talk as fast and as vehemently

as the 140 who had dispersed. They wanted to make their
own cranes or loading triangles and not be made to use the
slow, low-geared railway yard jib crane. They wanted
their own kind of tools, the tools they used in Portugal.
They would always be slow, working the British way with
strange tools. They wanted fish, dried ling, and rice, and
not the sort of rations they had been having. They wanted
fruit. They would buy oranges out of their own pocket.
They loved curries and the cooks should be able to make
them the kind of food they were used to go to work on.
They wanted no more bullying fat men with canes calling
them pigs and lazy dogs. They were civilised Portuguese,
and not cattle. The major would, however, be talking from
a gash in his throat if he insisted upon treating them as
they had been treated!

Jim Shaw had more than a grasp of psychology. He had
laboured in the forest. He knew how men toiled and how
they reacted to orders. He had taken orders and knew how
to give them. He knew about strange tools, foreign ways
and slow working. He cleared his throat and addressed the
interpreters. No one would bully them! They would get
exactly the tools they wanted, for he would see that the
blacksmith in Presteigne made what the Portuguese asked
for. He would instruct the ironmonger to supply the implements they needed. The Ministry would pay for them.
Furthermore, he would get on the telephone and see that
hundredweights of rice were shipped for them to make
their curries. There would be ling fish somewhere.

After they had been given permission to work in their
own way the Portuguese seemed a great deal happier.
They constructed their own crane or 'odd-legs' as they are
sometimes called, for three poles are generally employed.
The Portuguese, however, preferred four and their 'odd-
legs' were four-legged. The railway yard crane stood
motionless. The Portuguese were busy. They had their
own tools. They had dinner of dried ling, onions, rice,
curry. The tension seemed to have been relieved. What

pleased Jim Shaw was the progress made towards sorting
the great jumble of pitprops. It pleased the stationmaster
too, although he looked apprehensively for the fat man in
the British warm. The Portuguese looked for him too.
They heard him before they saw him. He began his barrage of oaths before he was properly on the scene. Jim
Shaw stood back and waited to explain that the pitprops
were actually getting stored in the trucks faster and more
efficiently than before.

'Heath Robinson!' shouted the fat man. 'Lazy so-and-
so's, the lot of them! We're not having this! The whole
thing is ridiculous!'

All at once Jim Shaw found one of his interpreters at his
elbow.

'Meester Shaw,' he asked, 'come and look, if you please,
at this pile of pitprops down here . . .'

The two interpreters had hitherto displayed a certain
demarcation in their spheres of liaison with authority. One
had dealt exclusively with work and tools for work, and
the other with the creature comforts of the Corps, and
complaints that were of a personal nature. It puzzled him
that the interpreter who urged him to come away down
the yard to look at timber was the one who normally talked
about fish and onions and curry. He was on the point of
asking what the trouble was when he looked back and saw
Major Cobbett being toppled from the top of the stack of
props by the jib of the odd-legs, swung with great force
and fascinating accuracy. The shouting and swearing had
suddenly ceased. Major Cobbett came down like Humpty-
Dumpty, crashing to the cinders where he lay, severely
shaken, badly bruised and lacerated. The Portuguese
stared blankly at him. Their teeth showed. Something
that was a Portuguese cheer went up to heaven. The work
of loading went on. Jim Shaw began to hurry to help the
fallen man and then changed his mind. The stationmaster
did likewise. Major Cobbett got slowly to his feet, like a
punch-drunk boxer, and made his way unsteadily down to

the office. It was useless to have an enquiry. The station-master himself claimed to have seen nothing. Jim Shaw could hardly recall what he had seen. Messrs Gomez and da Silva had seen nothing.

'Nothing, Meester Shaw,' they told him. 'Everybody busy working. Nobody looking. Accident. Unfortunate. Maybe the major have too much to drink, eh? Maybe his foot slip. Who knows, Meester Shaw?'

There was another score to be settled. Major Cobbett's underling, a certain Lieutenant Neal, was due to have his throat cut, it was hinted. When the insults had been atoned for, the record would be straight. Someone whispered a word in Lieutenant Neal's ear and he decided to accompany the major as his assistant in some new project, where foreigners had the sense to understand English and knew the scale of values that began, one Englishman, two Frenchmen, etc. etc.

It was as though the Corps had been transformed. The Portuguese proved themselves willing and co-operative. They worked with a will and smiled. What wasn't done one day would be done the next, of course, but men eating well and laughing while they worked was something Presteigne hadn't seen among the Portuguese since they had come. Extracting the timber from the woods they proved themselves good improvisers. They worked well with short-handled axes and the thumb-screwed fiddle saws. That they were hardy Jim Shaw had demonstrated to him one day when a man came to him displaying a raw, deep hack on his hand. The sufferer beckoned to him and went to a fire where his compatriots were burning an old pram tyre. At a nod two of them rose and held the man with the injured hand while a third, taking the burning pram tyre, applied it to the raw wound, filling it with melting rubber. The pain must have been excruciating. The Portuguese grinned at one another. The man whose hand had been 'treated' wiped the sweat from his brow, examined his palm, wiped it with the hem of his blue blouse, and went back to work. Jim Shaw asked one of the interpreters what it was all about. He was told that this was the common way of getting a deep wound on the hand to heal. The molten rubber both sealed and cauterised. Soon it would fall away or wear away. The scar tissue where the hack had been wouldn't break again. The man lost no time through what was really a minor disablement. The Portuguese were neither lazy men nor soft men. They were ready to work for their half-a-crown a day, despite all the slander the British officers had heaped upon them!

With things going better in the station yard Jim was able to get up to the Caen Woods and look at them with a more professional eye than he had done before. He sighed heavily at what he saw. There was only hardwood to come out of Caen Woods, mained oak and stool oaks, timber up to a maximum of ten inches in diameter. It was worth about ninepence a cubic foot and there was about 1,600 cubic feet of it to an acre. At thirty years it was a long, long way from maturity. It belonged to the children of the next generation when it might have amounted to four or five thousand cubic feet per acre even after being thinned, an asset worth thousands and thousands of pounds. There was no softwood, no larch or fir which would have done just as well for propping and shoring workings below ground. All that came out of Caen Woods went to the South Wales coalfield and the only economy in it all was that the short ends were usable as cogwood. This was done with interlaced columns of short timbers into the centres of which labourers would pour the spoil, making solid pillars for galleries in need of substantial support. The owners of Caen Woods were being robbed and exploited. The nation's resources were being squandered, and Jim Shaw and his Portuguese were themselves only cogs in the great wheel. They began to make more and more progress at Presteigne now. The norm had been four trucks of props a day. Now they shifted a trainload of twelve or fourteen trucks a day. Authority concerned with forms and consignment notes always gathers statistics. The difference was recorded. Frantic telegrams from pit managers slowed down and ceased. Somehow the lazy Portuguese had proved that they weren't lazy at all. Jim Shaw was very proud of them.

By this time the war was grinding on towards its climax. Jim Shaw heard the rumours and wondered about them from time to time, but he was somehow surprised when the news finally came through. He was admiring the neatness of the stacked timber at one end of the railway yard when there was a sudden shout from the other. Men stopped doing what they were doing, froze at the crane, in the trucks, on the tops of wagons. 'Armistice! Armistice! Armistice!' they yelled. A train whistle blew. Someone had rushed to toll a bell. The noise grew in volume. People stood and saw the world blur before their eyes as tears came. Some of the Portuguese crossed themselves and others went mad and began throwing the timber out of the wagons and the trucks.

Jim Shaw swallowed and thought of a great explosion in the brickfields at La Bassée as men he had marched with at Caterham died. The Portuguese couldn't know about that. They were civilians recruited to work in Britain and none of them had fought in the mud, or heard the frightening thunder of guns at Festubert and Loos. One of the wagons that had been emptied was trundled down the yard. Jim Shaw was seized by the jubilant Portuguese and hoisted up on top of it. They cheered him and laughed and slapped him on the back. He would drink with them at the Radnor Arms? He had no option but to allow himself to be propelled along. Presteigne, along with every larger and smaller place in Britain, was going mad that morning. Men were ardently kissing women and women were laughing and weeping at the same time. Publicans retreated behind the defence works of the bar and began to pull tankards of ale for which, in the height of their emotion, they asked no money. Soon, with all the talking, throats would become so dry that the beer would run out. Jim Shaw wasn't a drinking man. When he could extricate himself from the Portuguese and the locals he walked by himself and thought about tomorrow. He had made something of a reputation for himself with Professor Pritchard who had come down to look into things at Presteigne after the departure of the detested major. A quick-tempered and impatient man, Professor Pritchard's tolerance was reserved only for those who were efficient and got on with their job. He had commended Jim Shaw and a time would come when Professor Pritchard's path would cross Jim Shaw's again, with the same respectful outcome.

'It couldn't be for ever,' people were saying as they shook hands. 'We were bound to drive them back. Right was on our side!'

No one was as yet counting the cost except unimportant, practical fellows like Jim Shaw, who knew that a wood is a long time growing and when it is cut down neither the blessing of kings nor the lip-service of politicians talking of conservation will put it back again in a lifetime.

The war ended. The happy, relieved survivors recovered from their celebrations. The publicans mopped their floors and set stools and tables on their legs again. Jim Shaw was once again back in the railway yard seeing his Portuguese load the same sort of wagons with the same sort of timber to go down the line to the same mines. There was no change at first, except in the daily death roll. The pithead gear still wound and spun. The black-faced men still came up out of the hole. Ships still sailed with long black trails of smoke marking their progress across the horizon. Trains brought back the wounded. The pitprops were Jim Shaw's daily concern for three months more, even although the army had discharged him in December. He was now entirely in the service of the Ministry of Supply for the army paymaster had struck him off the payroll. By the end of February the Portuguese had lost all enthusiasm for labour in a foreign country. They were thinking of home. They worked half-heartedly. Everyone with a home to return to wanted to go there. Jim was thankful when his personal problem was solved for him. The Ministry decided that he could be better employed in a supervisory capacity on a government contract scheme handled by Messrs P. & W. Anderson Ltd, builders, of Piccadilly, London. They sent him to south-east London. He would be only a mile and a half from his wife's home. The project was the building of an Aeronautical Stores Depot in the shape of a plane hangar. He had to be content with this outlet for the time being. Many men who had been discharged from the army were content with much less. Many of them would be a long, long time finding suitable work of any kind.

Jim's work with the building contractors was concerned with timber, mainly the great pitch-pine beams which spanned the roof of the structure. That anything could go wrong on the site seemed impossible until one day, to the horror of the clerk of works and everyone else concerned with materials and blueprints, it was discovered that the great beams were all short by six inches. How could a roof be spanned when the beams were overall half a foot less than the total width of the proposed hangar? Rules were pulled from pockets and laid quickly end over end along the 14" × 10" pitch-pine timber. Jim Shaw stood and thought back to the lunchtime activity of some of the navvies on the site. He hardly dared voice his suspicion, and yet there could be no other explanation. Timber was being stolen for kindling wood. The navvies were quietly cutting themselves six inches off the beams and carrying it home in their dinner napkins.

A check proved this to be the case. Alas, a beam that must span between fifty and sixty feet isn't the slightest use when it is cut short. It can't be jointed. It must be intact, and able to carry the roof load. The dinnertime work with the saw had to come to an abrupt halt on that very day. Security saw to it that wherever the navvies' families found their morning kindling it wasn't on the hangar site!

While Jim was happy enough to have marked time at such work, he was far from content to remain in the city, or even in suburbia. He wanted to find a place in forestry. When the government contract ended he accepted with great enthusiasm a place with the Woodlands Valuation Company controlled by Dr A. H. Unwin, sometime Conservator of Forests in Nigeria, and a member of the publishing family of that name. Dr Unwin was a kindly man and quickly summed up the young forester's ability and ambitions. He badly needed a man who could select trees for felling and advise on replanting, someone who knew the sort of timber particular soils would best support, and above all, a practical forester able to supervise the extraction of trees when the company by which he was employed, undertook to find buyer or seller, and if necessary get the timber extracted for either party.

The work at Killearn and Skelmorlie had been invaluable training for general advisory work. Jim Shaw's success with the difficulty at Presteigne had added to his reputation. Dr Unwin had no hesitation in giving him a free hand in carrying out whatever commissions were passed on to him. The work would cover forests and woodlands on the borders of Surrey, Sussex and Hampshire. There was only one drawback, so far as Jim Shaw and his wife were concerned. He had to find his own accommodation. This meant renting or buying a house. Dr Unwin thought that Petersfield would be a pretty central place from which a timber adviser might operate. Jim Shaw listened to the advice and went home and told Edith about the new job.

'We'll be out of the town,' he said, happily. 'No more noise and dirt! We'll see green countryside, fields and woods, and great trees. We'll go down to Petersfield and see what we can find, that's if you agree with what I'm doing. . . .'

Edith Shaw smiled. She was in perfect agreement. She had hoped he would soon be away from the contractors and the hangar building. Such work wasn't the kind of thing a man with Jim Shaw's experience should be doing. Building with timber was for builders, for carpenters and joiners. Jim was a man of the trees, a forester. The sooner he got back to his proper environment the better. The Woodland Valuation Company sounded just the place for him. There was no telling where he might go from there. Already the government were waking up to the horror of depleted timber resources, and the prospect of a timber shortage that might last a generation or more. There was talk of planting on a great scale. Men with some knowledge of trees and sylviculture were being consulted. Sooner or later money would have to be spent on tree-planting.

7

Southern Woodlands

IT was good to be working out of doors, in his proper
element once more. A forester's life is always concerned
with the open air, with woods and the things that give
them life, water, air, good rich earth in which a seed can
germinate and grow to become a sapling tree. The rooms
they took at Petersfield were later to be exchanged for
others at Haslemere. Jim Shaw's first problem, after
settling for rooms when a house proved unobtainable, was
to meet a demand for a thousand poles, transmission poles
that had to be gleaned from the woods somehow or other,
if the Woodlands Valuation Company was to uphold its
reputation. Dr Unwin had optimistically promised to find
the poles. They had to be between 25 and 40 feet in
length with a minimum top diameter of six inches. The
woods were full of trees, or the remains of trees. There
were scrub trees a log-merchant might have been glad to
have, half-grown hardwoods that had somehow escaped
the greedy wartime merchants or their agents. There were
deciduous and conifer woods, but good clean poles were
like gold. Jim Shaw got on his motor-cycle and scoured
the countryside for them. He had an eye for good timber.
He could tell at a glance the sort of wood that might yield
the trees he wanted, but there was more to it. Owners of
woods were suddenly aware of the value of what remained

and reluctant to part with their good trees. It wasn't always
a simple matter of cutting down two or three tall larches.
Cutting would let in the wind, and the force of winter
gales could set ranks of good trees leaning on one another.
Even the most short-sighted man had discovered that a
tree took a long time growing and now had to be conserved
and looked after. A planter rather than a cutter-down of
trees, Jim Shaw understood only too well the problem he
was facing. He reproached his new employer with taking
on something that was proving almost impossible. When
he was quite desperate he found the last of his thousand
poles at Hindhead. They were a relic of some earlier tree-
felling folly, a batch of eighty lying out of the wind, supporting one another like drunken men in a football crowd.

'Whatever commission you accept for me,' he told Dr
Unwin, 'make sure you promise no more transmission
poles! I've hunted three counties for them. I never want
that kind of job again.'

Dr Unwin was careful not to accept the same kind of
offer again. He knew that Jim Shaw had scraped the
bottom of the barrel, and had heartaches when some of the
trees he had been compelled to buy had shown imperfec-
tions when they were barked.

'No more poles, Shaw,' he said. 'I promise you. We'll
find somebody that wants to grow timber instead of cut it
down.'

But of course, forestry is the business of planting, cultivating and harvesting. Trees grow and mature. There is a
time for planting and a time for pulling up that which is
planted as the Bible says. On Hawkley House estate they
loved their trees and conserved them as objects of beauty,
even although they were passing from being good mature
oak to be in some danger of rotting, as oaks will in their
later years. Summoned to advise on tree-planting, Jim
Shaw looked at the oaks. He smiled when he heard that
their owner was thinking of having his dining-room
panelled with foreign oak. What more fitting thing than to

use some of that fine estate oak, he suggested. It seemed
that no one had given it a thought, but the idea took hold.
The oaks were duly cut and made into boards, although,
by the time the timber was dried and aged, Jim Shaw was
too far away to see the sort of panels it made. Oak cut into
boards is best dried in the wind in a drying shed. It rests
on battens for perhaps two years before it is cut into panel
thickness and is then aged for three years more. When this
is done the man whose task it is to wax or French polish
the wood admires the medullary ray, that beautiful figur-
ing characteristic of the finest board. He works on it with
his beeswax and the softest pads of cotton wool and muslin
until the surface has the depth of plate glass and a wonderful purity of grain that no manufactured board can equal.

'A tree is beautiful growing to maturity, and beautiful
in its prime, but sad, and shameful when it rots and
becomes a shell,' Jim Shaw would remark. A great deal of
his work centred on the problem of replacing what had
been a harvesting business for generations in that part of
the world, coppice cutting. The coppice industry had not
only provided revenue for country estates for centuries, it
had provided work for a great variety of rural craftsmen
and still did. These men made baskets and clothes pegs,
fences and hurdles. From the ash coppice would come
material for hammer and axe handles, the shafts for agricultural implements, snare pegs, tent pegs and hop poles.
The hazel coppice provided thatching rods used on the
snugly thatched roofs of New Forest cottages, as well as
hurdles. In almost every coppice or clearing there would
be a faggot-maker. This was the last of the hey-day of the
village baker and faggots were in continual demand for
the bakehouse ovens where the bakers would brush away
the ash before they slid in their long wooden shovels of
kneaded dough. The faggot-maker tidied up every clearing and coppice so thoroughly that the crow could hardly
find a stick for a nest. In the oak coppice there would be
bark for the tannery. In the willow or osier beds, material

for basket-making-and wicker-weaving. Alder made soles for clogs. Birch made brooms for sweeping courts and paths, or leaf-strewn lawns in autumn.

Of all the craftsmen who worked away in the quiet places in the woods Jim Shaw was perhaps most fascinated by the hurdle-makers. They had practised their ancient craft for countless generations. It was all so seemingly simple and neat. The work was done where the hazel rods were longest and yet not too heavy and thick. They were expertly slashed apart and then split in two along their eight or ten feet until sufficient had been split to make one or two hurdles. The weaving couldn't be done without uprights. These were set in a specially drilled billet of wood which spaced them evenly along its length. Once these sharpened uprights were driven into the drilled timber the weaving went on at speed, tightly, evenly and endlessly. A man working for all he was worth could fashion almost three hurdles in a day. They were sold for three shillings and sixpence. The pay was perhaps not over-generous, but the farmers who kept sheep were far from prosperous. Agriculture was in as poor a state as forestry, even in the green and rolling country of the Downs.

Advisory work covered more than explaining how one kind of tree might shelter or nurture another. It entailed domestic problems such as cutting down trees that were unwanted or threatening life and limb. The axeman who had learned his craft in Killearn woods had lost none of his skill. Jim Shaw would stand and survey a group of eighty-feet larches or mammoth beeches and plan their felling even when there was barely room for them to lie where they must be brought down. He no longer scaled the trees himself, as he would have done before he was married. Now he was not only a husband but a father. His son, Donald, had been born in August 1921. An assistant was sent up to lop the branches, but Jim Shaw himself would check every stage of an operation that was to bring a giant down. Seventy-feet-high larches at Hindhead came down

as safely as tall beeches at Merrow, near Guildford, although
the larches gave cause for anxiety to at least one spectator.
One of these magnificent larches could only be felled
towards the porch of the house where it overlooked the
drive. The owner's brother, a gentleman who loved anything with an element of risk in it, sat on the porch offering
odds against the tree being felled without the insurance
company having to pay for damage. Jim Shaw stood back
and gauged the height of the tree, thinking of all the great
firs and pines he had dropped in the woods. Here it was
different. A foot or two of foliage might smash the porch
or bring down the doorway itself. Perched on the porch
was the Colonel in his chair. An audience puts many a
man out of his stride when something requiring critical
judgement is involved. Jim didn't need to check the height
of the tree. It would reach the porch. It might just bound
far enough to take the smile off the Colonel's cheery face
and it would be as well to persuade the gallant soldier to
retreat.

'If you don't mind, sir,' he said, ' I think we'll have you
moved back a little bit, say into the doorway, maybe into
the hall?'

The Colonel grinned. 'Ten to one you bring the porch
down. Five to one you block the door. . . .'

'Maybe,' said Jim Shaw and helped the Colonel to go
back as far as he would agree to go, into the doorway.

There was a moment or two of indecision and then Jim
Shaw looked at the towering column of that great larch tree
and nodded.

'Very well,' he said, clearing the saw and making the
last cut.

When a tree goes it often looks like the mast of a ship
being rolled on the swell of the sea, and then all at once,
almost before the loud cracking sound has died, it crashes.
Its branches rise again for an instant, like green waves.
The dust and stones beneath them are wafted back and
away. The great larch tree's tip swept the porch. Its

feathery top lashed down. The Colonel's smile had gone. He was thrown backwards. A doormat, blown into the air by the rush of wind, sailed over and fell on top of him!

The forester and his men hurried forward, clambered over the branches, and then smiled with relief.

'What odds now, sir?' they asked, laughing at last as the Colonel got to his feet and recovered his good humour.

No one dared think what might have happened had he remained sitting on the porch.

If the ash, hazel and oak coppice work was almost certainly going to decline and the trades associated with it cease to be practised, one kind of cropping would continue in that part of the world, for there the sweet chestnut flourished as in few other areas of Britain. Sweet chestnut is in most places regarded as an ornamental or amenity tree. Ordinary chestnut is not itself the most useful timber, although it may at one time have been sought after for making carts. The sweet chestnut has a particular weakness that generally makes it shunned by all save the fence-maker. It suffers from what the forester calls 'the shakes'. This trouble is harder to detect in a living tree than in man. In man it is visible. Its cause is equally evident. Shakes in a tree become apparent when it is cut down. Star-shakes, as they are called, radiate from the centre of the tree-trunk making it a wood to please the man who would split it down. Heart-shakes or cup-shakes, caused by the tree outgrowing its outer case, result in the heart falling out of the log, leaving it hollow like a tub. For this reason sweet chestnut is best harvested young. The fence-makers know how to cope with wood that splits easily. They cut it into 'pale' lengths and use some specially devised tools to split these 'pales' into stakes. A fromer is hammered in to the log to divide it into smaller and smaller sections. The resulting stakes are held in an improvised sawing horse armed with old saw blades so that they can be gripped firmly while they are smoothed with a draw knife. The 'pales' are sawn from trees up to twenty years old and the coppice left to regenerate. Any lengths of the tree unsuitable for splitting may be used as main fence supports. The stakes are wired into the fence at the mill and the fencing rolled for shipment to wherever it is needed. Small sections of chestnut coppice, round and as thick as a man's thumb, may be turned into walking sticks by steaming and bending, although steamed handles have a tendency to straighten on the first really wet day they are used.

Intrigued as he was by the fence-makers, Jim Shaw had to admit that much of what he had learned of their work would be of little use to him afterwards. This was a very local industry. Nowhere else would chestnut regenerate so readily to encourage the fence-maker. Soon he must move on. The Interim Forest Authority had been set up as long ago as 1919. Now the Forestry Commission was in being. Dr Unwin's enterprise had had official backing and a grant from the Government, but no politician would support a semi-private enterprise when money was being voted to the Commission to restore the country's timber resources and replant the thousands of acres of derelict woodlands.

Dr Unwin summoned Jim Shaw and explained the situation as far as he was concerned. He was going abroad as Conservator of Forests in Cyprus. The Woodlands Valuation Company might continue to operate, if Shaw was of a mind to take it on. It could be transferred to him and whatever connections it had would be his, but Jim Shaw was of a cautious disposition. He knew this would call for capital which he would have great difficulty in finding. Once again he was at the crossroads. Where was money being spent on reafforestation? Few estate owners had the means to invest in the future, planting the acreage of trees that needed to be planted and waiting for the investment to mature. Dr Pritchard, his mentor at Presteigne, had gone to the Forestry Commission and held a position of some importance there. He would write and

explain matters. Dr Pritchard had more than once suggested that the place for an experienced man with his background was in the service of the Commission.

'I seem to have come to the end of the line here,' he
wrote, 'and would be glad to hear if you happen to have a
situation available with the Commission. I am, after all, a
practical forester. I know the work, not from books and
the laboratory, but from having worked in the forest,
planting, thinning, harvesting. I can place the full details
before you, as I did for James Calder, to whom you may
care to refer. . . .'

Dr Pritchard needed no reminding. He needed men
like Jim Shaw and there were too few of them now and the
Commission in Scotland looked with a jealous eye upon
foresters lured south. College courses were producing
forest officers who could perhaps recognise blocks of
timber and tell ash from beech but some of them were
sadly behindhand at telling one living species of tree from
another.

'I am glad to hear from you, and pleased to be able to
offer you a situation as Forest Officer in charge at the South
Beat, Tintern and Chepstow Park. There is accommodation with the appointment. I am told that it is not all that
it might be, but every effort will be made to see that it is
brought up to standard. A better house may be provided
later.' Professor Pritchard hadn't inspected the accommodation at Tintern of course. Jim Shaw said that if his
wife would take it that the house was passable, all she
needed to do was to give the new job her blessing. Edith
Shaw didn't hesitate. They would move to Tintern. Jim
would become a civil servant.

Tintern, like the Forest of Dean and Alice Holt, was a
Crown Wood. It had, until the advent of the Interim
Forest Authority and finally the Forestry Commission,
been under the Office of Woods. It was a relic of the days
of the chase handed down through the ages and treated
with perhaps more consideration than privately owned

forests whose trees, according to the financial state of their owners, had often to be sacrificed to meet debts. A long-term policy of forest management had left the Crown Woods in a little better heart than others. Jim Shaw was to discover that his particular inheritance was at least the equal of some of the woods he had left, and in many ways much better, for any pattern of planting and cutting is better than none at all. It is true that he had to get out and plant. He busied himself to comply with the programme laid down by his new masters. He planted, thinned, cleared and even gathered acorns and went about making holes and popping them in. The crows religiously followed in his footsteps taking the acorns out again and it was soon made obvious that the crows of the southern woods were no less mischievous than those of Stirlingshire and Ayrshire. Not seriously disheartened, Jim carried on, putting in seedling oaks where he might have put in acorns. He planted hardwoods and conifers, a mixture of trees, remembering old Davy Carr's words of wisdom on the subject. When trees of different species are planted side by side the kind that does best on that particular soil will soon take over and no mixture result, the less virile species or the slower growing species being first dominated and then submerged by the tree that really thrives there. To overcome this natural tendency he would put in groups of four or five, instead of in ordered ranks of different species, content to lose three or even four to give the less prolific tree a chance. This kind of forest know-how would have to be explained, of course, to those who liked categorical order, not only on paper but on the forest floor. If only God can make a tree the forester who plants it has some responsibility for seeing that it gets a chance to flourish.

The work out of doors went well enough. It was, after all, a world to which Jim Shaw had been born and bred. Indoors Edith Shaw was less content. The Cot, Chepstow Park, had a rather grand-sounding name that belied its true condition. It was little more than a derelict. It was

damp and Jim had to admit that he had seen more comfortable forest bothies. Perhaps it was a sort of heirloom
from the days of the chase. A forest keeper had been its
tenant. There may have been a day when the sometime
Surveyor of Woods had considered it fit for habitation but
Jim Shaw, his modern counterpart, knew that his family
was so ill-housed that they could not suffer the hardship
for long without endangering their health. He spoke to his
superiors about it and was asked to be patient. Foresters
have to be patient. There is no other philosophy in the
management of woods that will serve than one of tolerance
and patience. Nothing happens from day to day. The
forester who can check the growth of a tree in less than a
year knows that the full cycle of the seasons must be past
before he can draw any useful conclusion. The cycle of the
seasons was passing at Chepstow Park. A little longer and
we'll see what is to be done, the Shaws told one another. A
little longer, but not for ever in a derelict of crumbling
plaster and rising damp and insanitary conditions.

Out of doors again Jim Shaw went about meeting
the people that the forest supported, the contractors, the
minor tradesmen buying wood for different purposes, the
log trade, the country joiners, the builders and farm contractors and that disappearing race, the descendants of the
very ancient industry of charcoal burning. There had been
charcoal burners in the Chase since the days of William
Rufus. They still carried on in the Forest of Dean and in
Tintern, working in the hidden-away clearings where their
ancestors had worked, at the old charcoal pits The method
now was less wasteful than in William's time. In his day
the burners had simply tumbled furze and brushwood into
a pit, piled on the billets once the fire was going well and
then heaped over it all a green covering of branches and
finally soil through which the blue smoke would curl for
days on end until the wood was carbonised and the pit
could be uncovered and raked out. In Tintern and Dean
they built their charcoal mounds with great care and skill.

If they could find a sheltered place they were happy. It had to be close to the particular kind of wood producing the kind of charcoal that was needed. Oak was favourite but alder had always pleased the makers of gunpowder. Oak, of course, was easier got and pleased the smelters or the smithies where charcoal was still in demand.

Making a charcoal mound had nothing haphazard about it for it must be symmetrical, of a given height and base area and contain ventilation apertures capable of being opened or stopped up according to the force and direction of the wind. A charcoal burner watches the mound with the greatest care and never leaves it from the time it is first ignited until it is smothered for cooling down The wood or the charcoal embers must never really burn but slowly undergo the chemical change brought about by the distillation of the sap in the wood. At first the mound sweats. The smoke rises and spirals and curls and drifts away. It burns like a dying fire and then as the first combustion results in the exact degree of heat that is needed the watchful charcoal burners will fuss around the source of their living as anxiously as cooks preparing a banquet. After it has sweated it will breathe. Its core will be radiant with a heat that would make iron flow. The breathing will be wisps of a beautiful blue colour and the process will go on day after day, no matter what the weather. The owl will look down at it, the hunting fox sniff the air and perhaps come and inspect it at a distance, aware of the charcoal burners taking turns to keep a watch. It is a silent world, a world of moonlight at one part of the month and complete blackness when the moon no longer rides the sky. The burning does nothing to stop the frost on the carpet of old dead leaves or the boundary fence. It scents the air or makes it pungent and day comes, wears on and grows old while the charcoal burners cook their food and go in and out of their hut or improvised shelter thinking not of the crowing of the cock pheasant or the cooing of pigeons but of the rustling of dead leaves on the autumn trees perhaps, and the possibility of the wind getting up. Their perfect weather is the kind in which couch grass smoulders or mounds of leaves refuse to break into flame but keep the fire that was lit in them on a damp afternoon when the man who burned them is long gone.

In the end the burners take their shovels and cap and coat the mound with damp or wet soil, covering it evenly to exclude the slightest amount of air. The heat gradually dies. They carefully inspect their product and nod their approval if the grains are sound and even and have that almost iridescent metallic sheen that the best charcoal must have. It has yet to be sieved or graded, bagged and taken away. The business tends to make a man's hands and face black and makes him cough when the dust reaches his lungs. Time is less important than the care that is taken in dealing with the charcoal residue when the mound finally disintegrates and becomes a mere heap. In the beginning it was a work of art built round a central pole from which the base logs radiated like a cart wheel. The heavier lengths of wood were packed upright around the central pole, graded so that the larger diameter of cordwood was situated where the heat would be greatest. Four tons of cordwood built into the cone or mound might leave a ton of charcoal.

There was still one domestic purpose for which charcoal was in demand when Jim Shaw was at Tintern. Industrious ladies who took a pride in their ironed sheets would buy charcoal for their smoothing irons. The charcoal burners had no time to sell penny lots. Their market, although it was rapidly declining, was one that took the product in hundredweights or ten or more bags at a time. Local lads who thought to make a shilling or two would keep an eye on the charcoal burners and when the weary, much dried-out men went to sleep in a more comfortable bed or quench their thirst at the pub, the villains would steal from the mound, hastily filling sacks with the stuff the burners had laboured so long to produce. The thievery

greatly incensed the old charcoal burners. It wasn't only
that they had sat up night and day for five or six days but
they had cut cordwood of from three to five inches diameter
into two-foot lengths for weeks on end. It takes a lot of
work with saws and axes to make the thing worthwhile.
They would complain to the police and the Forest Officer
that the fruits of their labour were being stolen. Jim Shaw
sat up and kept watch for the thieves. He had done this
kind of thing many times and kept long vigil for tree
thieves, poachers, and now charcoal thieves. On this
occasion the watch was successful and the culprits taken
black-handed at the mound. Perhaps it was the uncer-
tainty of supplies that made women discard the charcoal
iron that kept its heat and renewed its glow by the
simple process of being pushed up and down a fine linen
sheet.

When personal discomfort could be tolerated no longer
Jim Shaw made his final protest. He was leaving the house
that still remained the derelict it had been when he and his
wife moved in. It was impossible to continue living there,
he said. He was up and away this time and no soft words
would persuade him to do other than get out. Like a lot of
outdoor men he was slow to anger but when he made up
his mind to do a thing it was firmly made up.

'I have no alternative but to move out,' he told those in
authority. 'I have drawn attention to the unsatisfactory
conditions in which my wife and child have had to live for
a year now. I am going and nothing will persuade me to
remain!'

The hitherto persuasive gentleman looked at Jim Shaw
and saw that he had red in his eye. Here was a man who
had jumped off the top of the highest firs, dealt with a
bullying army officer, to say nothing of his days in the
Guards.

'He seems to be set to go' they said. 'We'd better have a
word with Professor Pritchard. After all, he got him to
come here.'

Professor Pritchard was put out to discover that Jim Shaw had the bit between his teeth. If things hadn't worked out there was hope that they could be made to work out. A better house, perhaps, but there wasn't a suitable house and Jim Shaw was in no mood for waiting.

'I think the place for you might be North Wales, Shaw,' said Professor Pritchard. 'There doesn't seem to be much hope of the present house being put in order while you are in it.'

Jim Shaw said amen to that. He had never seen less done to a place and it seemed The Cot would fall down before the Commission got round to doing some work on it or engaging a contractor to do it for them.

'North Wales?' he said thoughtfully.

He remembered his wife talking of the tragic death of a Forest Officer in North Wales.

'Wouldn't it be odd,' she had said,' if instead of putting The Cot right they sent you up there?'

'Betws-y-Coed?' he asked.

'In Caernarvonshire,' said Professor Pritchard who loved Wales. 'One of the beauty spots of the north,' he went on, 'beside the River Conway. Up there you will be expanding the existing woodland and planting hundreds of acres of newly acquired land, whole mountainsides, clearing scrub, heather, gorse. You'll like it up there. You'll get on well with the people they're Celts, like yourself . . .'

They were Celts at Tintern of course, but Jim Shaw didn't care to take issue with the Professor over a detail.

'And accommodation?' he said. 'I must have something a great deal better than we have here. My wife has been a good, patient, wife to me and she deserves something better than I have been able to give her so far.'

'A choice,' said Professor Pritchard. 'A choice of four houses, one of them a brand new one to be built.'

They couldn't live in a house that was yet to be built but

again Jim Shaw, mollified by the Professor's solemn promise, was disinclined to quibble about being able to live in a blueprint or in a picture postcard of the Swallow Falls on the Llugwy. He liked the idea of the mountains and the tracts of heather and wilderness from which he might raise his own forest and live to see it mature.

'I'm offered the Forest Officer's job at Betws-y-Coed,' he told Edith. 'The Professor says we have a choice of four houses, one of them a new one being built.'

Edith smiled. She was ready to go. She was that kind of woman. They looked at the map and saw the mountains marked upon it, Snowdon and the Glyders, Tryfan, the Carnedds, and nearer to hand, Moel Siabod dominating Capel Curig.

'What is there there?' she asked.

'From what I gather,' said Jim, 'small-holdings, sheep, old lead workings, a few mountain lakes and a lot of heather and whins. A whole wilderness to be planted in time, not an already established pattern like Chepstow and Tintern and not the soft country around Haslemere and Petersfield. It probably rains a lot more up there than it does here. The soil will be washed off the slopes, I expect, and maybe the small-holders won't give us very much of a welcome when we have to turn them off old grazings. We'll see. I expect they teach the children in Welsh up there so when Donald goes to school he'll have to learn the language. What do you say?'

'Whatever you want,' said Edith.

Jim Shaw confirmed his acceptance of the posting to North Wales and took his family up there with little or no regrets. Life had always been a battle of one sort or another and he was prepared for that. It was what a man expected, although as they travelled north Jim Shaw could have little idea of the enormous task that would confront him for years as he went out to do something even his grandfather had never had to do, plant his own forest, establishing it, winning land from the wild, fencing in and enfolding in the forest, people and their homes, cottages, small-holdings and lead workings some of them long abandoned and some still being worked by the miners.

It was 1924. Betws-y-Coed hadn't become the Mecca of the tourist yet. It was peaceful and unspoilt and the river flowed quietly through shingle banks on which cattle often stood swishing their tails to discourage the flies.

8

Good Years and Bad

THERE were no flies to bother the cattle along the river-bank when the Shaws came to that part of North Wales, nor were the shingle banks exposed. The river was high in the tidal reaches and backing up despite the flood of water from the uplands. Jim Shaw strained his eyes for a glimpse of the forest he was to manage, not sure where it would begin or end but he could see nothing. It was dark. If the forest was there it lay in the shadow of the valley walls and merged with the background of the night. Rain obscured the compartment windows as the train trundled on its way to Betws. The forester lowered a window and sniffed the night air, the smell of wet grass, a whiff of woodsmoke and then the acrid smoke of the engine as it changed course a little, following the river. He rubbed the grit from his eyes and withdrew his head. On the other side of the valley a lamp-lit place slid by, like a pleasure steamer travelling through the night. It was Dolgarrog, huddled below the mountain. Soon afterwards the train came to a halt at Llanwrst. A porter with rain dripping from his cap called, 'Lla'wrst, Lla'wrst,' a door banged and voices of people speaking in Welsh slowly diminished in volume. The train hissed steam. The platform lamp glimmered in the rain and time stood still, as it always does when a man sits in a train, not knowing quite when his journey will be over, and the engine driver talks with the guard or the porter.

'Now sit still, Donald,' Jim Shaw told the boy. 'It won't be long now.'

It already seemed like an eternity to them all, for the trip from South to North Wales by rail is long and slow, encompassing the principality and exaggerating its dimensions. When they moved out of Llanwrst Jim Shaw noticed the glimmer of light on the river and the blackness of the valley moved in again. It wasn't far to Betws now. They would soon be there, and then all at once they were. They looked down at the platform, saw the stone buildings in the gloom and a partly-obscured light that marked the entrance to the station.

'At last, at last,' he said. Jim Shaw opened the door and looked for Mr Broadwood, the District Officer who had preceded him to Betws from Tintern Forest. As he stepped down and helped his wife to alight he could hear the rushing of the river not far away. It was part of a background of sound that was flood and rain in the dying leaves of deciduous trees, rain that dripped into puddles and made them radiate light and glitter for a brief moment before they became black again. A bare three weeks later this wet autumn would overfill the catchment of Llyn Eigiau and burst the dam above Dolgarrog, but Jim Shaw hadn't heard of Eigiau and knew nothing of the peat bed that this night's rain was helping to wash from under the dam's foundation. Mr Broadwood shook his hand and greeted Mrs Shaw and the boy. They followed him thankfully, feeling less like strangers for his presence, and the warmth of welcome.

Edith Shaw wondered about the people on the street and where they all came from. They were Saturday shoppers down from the hills to collect their boxes of groceries, their oil and candles, tea, soap and matches. Most of them would, after an hour or two's conversation, plod back again to their remote holdings, one or two meeting at chapel perhaps, the following day.

'How much farther?' the small boy asked again. He was taking good care of his dog and anxious to have this seemingly endless journey over.

They found their accommodation for the night, had their meal and were soon abed. For a short time Jim Shaw lay awake listening to the torrent of water frothing through the rocks, and the rain spattering now and then across his window, then he slept. The little town of Betws-y-Coed had taken its name from the wood. It sleeps among trees, oaks that have inspired many an artist along the river's course. Two hundred years before foresters lower down would fell and float their trees to Conway, fine Welsh oaks from a green and fertile valley. Jim Shaw had come to plant trees and do what he could to reclothe the mountain before peat was washed away and what soil there was followed it into the river. It was no task for a faint-hearted man. In the light of day, when a cock was crowing to a clearer morning sky, he looked up at the hillsides and began to see the magnitude of the thing. A thousand trees would barely patch the smaller areas of devastation. A year wouldn't be enough to clear the toppings and loppings, or tackle the growth of coppice springing up wherever war-time felling had taken the crop.

'Do you know what they say about this place?' he said to Edith as they took their breakfast.

'That it is one of the beauty spots of Wales,' she answered.

He smiled wryly. 'Oh it's that. No, they say that the forest stinks because it is plagued by three things. With sheep that can't be kept out of the trees. With rabbits that nibble away at every transplant a man puts in . . .'

'And the third thing?'

'Untrained labour! Mr Broadwood tells me that I have only one forest-trained man, the foreman. All the rest are small-holders, sheep men, miners.'

How would he manage? He only knew that somehow he would manage. Sheep could be kept out with wire. Rabbits could be snared and shot and trapped. Foresters could be trained. Everything had to have a beginning. He needed a map. There wasn't one. He needed to see how well things that were supposed to have been done were done. Mr Broadwood would let him have his map. He would look in whatever files there were to see what had been planted and where.

'We'll see the house as soon as possible and when our things come we'll move in. I must get on,' he said. 'You only need half an eye to see that this will become a losing battle in a couple of years unless the mess is cleared up.'

His predecessor had been fighting the coppice and trying to plant at the same time, but aftergrowth and undergrowth makes much faster progress than any transplanted tree. Once coppice growth gets out of hand clearing it becomes more and more difficult.

Mr Broadwood's map showed the extent of the acquired land and the boundary of the old-established woodland. Jim Shaw began to think that he must begin where Davy Carr had set him to work as a boy, in the nursery, raising the seedlings with which he might plant the plateaux away above the present tree-line, in the wilderness of heather and peat and roundrush. He would need an endless stock of Sitka spruce and Norway spruce. He would need larch and pine, and maybe silver fir and Douglas fir, noble pine, and even, before it was done, redwood from California. This was to be his life's work, he told himself, and one day he would live under the tall trees he had planted, for every year there would be growth and improvement. The Commission might not be able to please the amenity critics, but it would make use of its Treasury grants and show a return on the money with thinnings. The thinning would produce revenue for more and more planting, and one day, in suitable places the public would have oak-tree shade and smooth-trunked beeches as fine as any to be seen in the north.

A spell inspecting the tools and equipment and Jim Shaw was free to go and look at his enemies, the vagrant, wandering forest sheep and the multitude of rabbits. There were hundreds of the former, and hundreds of thousands of the latter, or so it seemed. The drystone walls of the old forest had been built up here and there and pushed down again by the owners of the sheep. In the quiet corners of the forest old, shaggy ewes with no brand-marks stood on their hind legs and browsed on foliage or barked the saplings. There were sheep tracks that were a vast network impossible to define. No dog could ever have rounded up so many 'wild' sheep. Some were probably ownerless. Some had hardly ever been out of the forest and were native to the ground, like the wild goats in Snowdonia. Jim Shaw studied the problem and decided that the walls would all have to be made good. The work would be budgeted for under the heading of fencing. Coppice-cutting would be higher on the list than planting. Rabbit clearance? He sighed at the impossibility of this task, for who could keep down creatures that were capable of breeding from the age of six weeks, and would produce litters almost the whole year round excepting perhaps the months of December and January? A keeper was needed or a rabbit trapper.

'They spoke the truth about the rabbits and the sheep,' Jim Shaw told his wife that night. 'You wouldn't believe how agile those sheep are and if you ask me their owners do all they can to put them into the forest rather than keep them out. As for the rabbits, the very ground moves with them in some places, like fleas on the back of an old dog.'

'Then we'll have rabbit and mutton stew,' said Edith Shaw but Jim Shaw barely smiled. He was thinking of his third problem and the accommodation available for them when his labourers and lead miners were turned into forestry men.

'Nice enough lads,' he said. 'Willing enough, but dear me, I could do with half a dozen of my father's old hands, then we might get on.' Men like Davy Carr weren't being turned out any more, however. There were no Davy Carrs or Buchanans to be hired, only small-holders whose experience of caring for anything was reflected in the behaviour of the long-coated, wayward sheep.

The planting programme had to be curtailed that year. There was no help for it. A march needed to be stolen on the coppice growth before a planting target could be achieved. The wall-building was tackled with enthusiasm. The small-holders beyond the pale either let their sheep in or encouraged them to climb the walls which most self-respecting Welsh mountain sheep find second nature. Jim Shaw was convinced that the sheep could fly. No matter how well the walls were built the trespass continued. He reinforced the walls with fences and barbed wire and the sheep that were on the outside were prevented from getting in except when some old and crafty ram led a company intent upon homing to the woods. Occasionally some hill walker would encounter a small flock of sheep standing by a gate and innocently let them in. The same sheep would hastily trot away if any member of the forest staff approached them at the gate. They knew their guilt. It had been instilled in them by their equally crafty owners. This, and a natural instinct to return to the terrain of their infant nurture, made them a continual nuisance to the forester. Inside they browsed their way across hundreds of young trees and Jim Shaw was half inclined to suggest that the Commission hired a butcher rather than a rabbit trapper. One old ram, picked up and transported for life, it was hoped, quickly turned about and jog-trotted miles along the road to get back to Gwydyr. If the battle against the sheep was being won sometimes it looked as though it must go on for ever.

When the sheep were thoroughly banished from the planted areas, Jim Shaw was dismayed to discover that as

forest animals or browsers among the heather and brambles they had been doing one useful thing. They had been
continually cropping down seedling gorse. With no sheep
to cut it back the young gorse rose to choke out the newly-
planted trees. A season revealed the new problem. Men
had to be drafted to cut back and clear the gorse crop
before the Sitka could rise above it and win. The men who
weren't clearing coppice and brambles were either cutting
out the gorse or making draining channels so that trees
could grow on hitherto waterlogged areas of the new
plantations.

'We will win in the end,' said Jim Shaw. 'It is all a matter
of applying knowledge, experience, like that fellow over
the top there who has fenced his pigs on the heather so
that they have nothing else to do but root it up. He tells
me that when they have cleared the ground, as they are
doing just as effectively as men would have done it, he
will scatter the residue of seed from his haycrop on it and
have a new pasture for his cow.'

Not every small-holder in the forest had the same
acumen but the plan worked. The pigs rooted out and
chewed up the heather roots. The winnowed hayseed,
liberally scattered on the black earth, took root and in the
following summer milking cows were grazing on the
young grass and consolidating an oasis in the wilderness.

Jim Shaw's concern was for many things not normally
the work of a head forester. He had inherited forest farms,
between fifteen and twenty of them sizeable holdings,
stocked with sheep, milking cows, store cattle, pigs and
poultry. This brought upon him the responsibility of a
Factor or Agent. When any of the forest farms needed
maintenance it was to the forester the tenants went. He
would see that they got a new roof, a better well, an improved shippon or barn. He saw to their gates, their fences,
their bridges, and was thankful that all this had been part
of his training at Killearn. While he was attending to the
needs of the tenants of farms he was also supervising work

on the old buildings and cottages within the acquired land, places due to be renovated for workers. He even found time to pipe water from the well in his own garden. The house in which he and his family had settled was to be occupied temporarily, but they went on living there for six years. What mattered most to Jim Shaw was the planting programme. He would have a forest of 16,000 acres and millions of trees when the whole task was accomplished but there was a long, long way to go, and even the most careful planning can hardly take account of natural disasters like gale damage and fire. The tallest trees in Gwydyr had fallen not far from the castle which had given the forest its name. They were carefully measured—135 feet. Trees on the uplands had failed to make growth because the land was so exposed to the prevailing wind, funnelled by the Snowdon ridges on one side and Moel Siabod on the other, and because, in one plantation, the land was acid beyond expectation. The young trees here grew only four inches in fourteen years and remained a monument to the unsuitability of the land, the species, and a system of planting that emphasised numbers of seedling trees put in rather than growth.

'One day,' said Jim Shaw, 'old Davy Carr promised me the sun would shine on me. I remember him saying it as I was kneeling in the nursery, weeding. I was sixteen. I am still waiting for it to shine on me here at Gwydyr!'

He had been planting for a decade and more. The people who took the A5 through from the Conway valley to the valley of the Ogwen river could see the great carpet of trees, the soft green of larch in early summer, the dark green of pine, the different shades of spruce and silver fir. Already contractors were in, taking thinnings. The forest was yielding a small harvest of pitprops and rustic poles, Christmas trees and the material for fences and gates. The lead miners had gone their way. For the most part they hadn't made very satisfactory foresters. The small-holders had proved a little more amenable to training, but there was now a generation of young foresters, trained in the art of clearing, planting, thinning, felling, and taught how to drain slopes, extract timber and so on. They worked with the contractors and listened to the advice that Jim Shaw had to give when they turned to him with a problem. A hundred times Jim Shaw blessed his early training at Killearn and wondered what the old men he had served under would think of Gwydyr could he have shown it to them.

By 1938 the Commission had been in control of Gwydyr for nineteen years. Even conifer trees take more than twice as long to reach a really productive stage but Gwydyr was looking good and in that very dry spring the hearts of the men planting and working in the forest were light and happy. Down in the valley the wild duck flew. On the moorland the curlew called. The cuckoo would come, as it always did, in May, calling on its way up the lonely mountain cwm and alighting now and again on a rock. God was in his heaven that spring, and perhaps all that he needed to do to make heaven on earth was to send a little gentle rain each day, enough to make the seedling tree grow a better root, to make the bluebell spring and the fronds of fern unroll, to put a little water in the stream and save the fingerling trout from dying for lack of oxygen. There had been a spring fire by April. Fires were a drought risk almost every year but Snowdonia is normally a comparatively high rainfall area, and a drought of ten days produces no anxiety except to the forester whose plantations are exposed to both the wind and the sun. When this is the case it needs only a fragment of broken glass to focus a smouldering ray. The wind fans the small flame and fire runs. They had long before stocked the roads and rides with beaters' brooms and fire-fighting utensils. It was common forest practice. There was a fire-warning horn. Everyone was well aware of the danger of an outbreak. It would have been impossible to guess where fire would come if it did. Jim Shaw could only content himself that if fire did really take hold he could cope with it. 1938 was, however, the driest spring experienced in the history of the forest. The streams had dried up. Beneath boulders soil had crumbled away. There was no moisture near the surface and things that had begun to shoot up had dried out and died. Every day the level of water in the mountain lakes fell lower. The up-land grazings provided little for the sheep that were ranging over them. Fishermen in Llanwrst put away their rods and resigned themselves to waiting for the spate that would have to come before the salmon run.

Jim Shaw was in the habit of drawing the wages for his staff at the bank in Llanwrst at this time. He would go down after the bank closed and receive the money from the manager in his private office. Mrs Shaw went with him and enjoyed the outing. It was particularly pleasant down in the valley that day in May. The sun shone. The riverside meadows were yellow with buttercups. The swallows had come and were darting above the tallest trees, taking the flies hatched in the stagnant water of streams and ditches. The sunlight glittered on the ripple of water barely covering the gravel of the riverbed and a train was winding its way from Bettws to Llanwrst.

They were driving back home when Jim Shaw caught a glimpse of what he took to be smoke cloud on the far side of the river.

'Is that smoke up there?' he asked.

His wife looked at the smoke and considered it for a moment.

'Yes,' she said, 'but it has carried on the wind. A train has just passed and it is probably smoke from that you can see.'

Jim Shaw's instinct for this kind of thing was uncanny. He knew the very colour of smoke from a burning tree. It wasn't pale and thin like train smoke being dissipated by the breeze. It was like the smoke from the tabernacle in the wilderness, like smoke from a sacrificial mound. He pulled up abruptly.

'No, it's not smoke from the train, my dear,' he said. 'The forest is burning! That's smoke from trees on fire up at Aberllyn.'

The smoke column rose almost as he spoke, and he knew how the fire would run, feeding on the dry herbage, wafting through under bushes and jumping over waterless draining channels. Sparks would ride on the wind and fall to supplement the blaze. The front would broaden with the change in the contour of the slope.

'I've got to get up there right away!' he told his wife. 'You must get to a telephone and get help. This isn't a little blaze. This will go like a wave!'

Neither of them stopped to wave or look back. Mrs Shaw hurried to find the nearest telephone, glancing up at the hills every so often and wondering how it had started. No one needed to tell her what the drought meant in these circumstances, or how urgent it was to get men to the scene of the fire. There were forestry workers on call but she knew they would either be on their way or already there. Smoke over the hill produced the same anxiety in every one of them. None wanted to see the fruits of his labour destroyed. The telephone was already busy. People were ringing up to find if it was serious, and was the fire brigade on the way? Volunteers were being marshalled. Mrs Shaw called the labour corps upriver and rang the District Officer. Before the afternoon was out they would need help from other forests and the army would be asked to send troops, for already trees were being consumed at the rate of five hundred a minute. A half million trees and transplants would be destroyed before it was over. The lark sang above the meadows and people on the road stopped to say what a wonderful afternoon it was. They could smell burning gorse. It is a fragrant smell, as much a part of the spring of the year and early summer as the smell of burning leaves in autumn.

Jim Shaw was driving as fast as he could up the rough road to the High Parc area of Gwydyr Forest. Grit spurted from the wheels of his car and he hoped that he would meet nothing coming down. He had no time to lose. Every minute the blaze would gain ground. Every minute it needed someone beating it to death in the stalks of bracken or gorse and the smouldering peat below. The wind was carrying the pall of smoke high and wide. The curtain of sparks that went with it rose on the hot air and crossed the valley road, and the valley itself. Later in the day flecks of ash would meet travellers on the road far out of sight of the forest and they would smell the fire in the air.

The spade Jim Shaw had brought with him was something he always carried in the car. He was soon using it for all he was worth, beating down flames, shovelling earth on smouldering debris. He coughed and cleared his throat, tore off his tie, opened his shirt, and got on with the job until sweat ran into his red-rimmed eyes and he was almost on the verge of exhaustion. The sun seemed to have got hotter but this was a back wave of heat from a fire front a mile wide. The flames climbed up tall gorse and made it collapse around charred stalks and a moment later a fresh wave of fire would do the same thing in the next planting. The rabbits that ran on were pursued. Those that dived into the earth were suffocated. The small birds rushed away and the raven sailed out to cross the valley and escape the cloud of smoke. The buzzard's perch fell in ruin and the buzzards mewed as they headed back from the blackened, smouldering ground that had been a spruce planting.

By nine o'clock that night the fire was proving master of the field. Its roar was frightening and discouraging for the men who hoped to stop it turning at the end of a lake, for their efforts were futile, Flame died on one side of the water. Hot air carried the sparks 150 yards to the other. Forest cottages seemed in danger. The fire was fought on a dozen fronts. Its main advance was as irresistible as the waves of Prussians Jim Shaw had watched coming into the brickfields of La Bassée. At the old mine workings the

fences were charred. At the still operating mine at Parc
the explosive store was in danger. Men rushed to move
dynamite from the threatened store, and others, who knew
nothing of the danger of explosion rubbed the grit and
grime from their brows and thought of the pints of bitter
they would order at one of the pubs down in the valley.
Mrs Shaw and the women of Aberllyn had been busy
preparing food and taking it to the men who were beating
the flames. It was a task almost as big as controlling the
fire. There were four hundred men now, and the battle was
still being lost. People who had watched the pall of smoke
could now see the very course of the blaze, for it was dark.
Sparks rose when a tree fell. The fire danced a wild dance
and the faces of the men who were nearest to it were
bright red.

'A thousand trees?' suggested a reporter enquiring of
Mrs Shaw.

The forester's wife had no time for idle questions and
futile speculation. It was a good part of her husband's
labour that was going up in smoke. It was a harvest that
should have been gathered by another generation.

'You will be able to judge for yourself when they get it
out!' she said, praying that they could achieve as much
while there was still a plantation left. At three o'clock in
the morning men with shirts holed by sparks blackened by
charcoal longed for their beds and wondered how much
longer they could keep at it. Someone had said half a
million trees. It was a nightmare—Dante's inferno, with
no escape for the tormented.

The people of the valley had slept the night through.
Day was coming and the fire still burned. It had been
burning for fourteen hours and it seemed that only a
miracle could quench it. Jim Shaw saw the morning sky
and shrugged his shoulders, feeling cooler for a moment
and wondering if he had caught a chill or a dew had fallen.
He touched his brow with his hand and it was moist. The
spade he picked up again was damp to his touch. All at

once he knew that the moisture in the air, the change in the wind, and the progress of the fire were connected. It was the mist that often crept off the high mountains in advance of rain. Condensation on the mountain was followed by rain. In a little while, with the help of Providence, rain would begin to make the ground smoulder a little more. Steam would suffocate the embers, raindrops kill the fire on the ground, and halt the blaze like an express train being pulled up.

'It will rain in the next hour,' he prophesied shakily. 'We'll have it under control with any luck. We'll be able to get out of here and lie down and rest!'

The rain was rising again in steam by seven o'clock as he had predicted. It began to quench the fire. Great stumps that had rolled from slopes where the soil had burned down to fine sand, began to smoke as they were penetrated by the warm rain. Men rubbed their faces and felt the rawness of scorched cheeks, lacerated arms and hands. Their boots had shrunk and hardened and they were like miners coming up from a pit after a disaster. Jim Shaw began to gather news of the fire from the different parts of the High Parc where men had been labouring on through the night. It was finished. It was beaten. If they hadn't beaten it to death they had fought it until the rain had drowned it, and the beast was dead.

'I think I'll sleep for a week,' Jim Shaw said as he went and found his car to drive home. He almost fell asleep at the wheel. It had been one of the longest nights of his life, and he couldn't think what he had been doing before the fire began. The smell of burning was in his clothes and his hair. It was in his lungs like a whiff of gas and his breathing was painful.

'If anybody wants me, anybody but one of the staff,' he said, 'tell them I'm in bed and I won't be getting out of it until tomorrow.'

Up on the High Parc more than four hundred acres of blackened and burnt-out plantation would remain a scar on the landscape for a long time. It would be nearly twenty years before the scar was healed and the trees clothed the ground once more.

A tree bends before the wind, or it breaks and is a tree no more. A man too, bends to his fate and his resilience allows him to survive. They were soon restoring the High Parc land, setting transplants between the rows of charred and dead trees that the fire had left. It takes a long time to replant so many trees and keep a forest expanding and thriving as it should. The conifers had gone and were replanted. Other things had gone too, of course, the undergrowth, the brush, the hazel thicket, the bilberry bushes and bog myrtle. The food of larvae that would hatch from the recovering earth. All at once Jim Shaw found himself contending with a minor plague where the fire had raged. The hazel weevil found no hazel upon which to browse, and, instead, fed on the freshly-planted spruce. It took a month or two to win this battle and contain the pest. Jim Shaw was nothing if not resilient. He tackled the scorched ground as enthusiastically as he had laid out its planting in the first place. He was never a defeatist. The swings and roundabouts were not symbolic of the futility of man's efforts to overcome nature. A man who worked hard and knew what he was doing would always reap his due reward. It was important to think this way. Forestry was not a natural happening. It was as one-sided as cultivating wheat on a field where thistles or thorns had flourished. It was as important to overcome setbacks as to win a war.

There was talk of war in 1938 and more still in 1939. No one had promised the Kaiser a birthday present, but Hitler was threatening to help himself. That war would come was daily more and more apparent. When it did they would need timber as they had always needed it, for pit-props and transmission poles, for masts and gates and fences, and even for barricades. They would come and get it as they had always done, oak for the men-of-war, oak for railway sleepers, poles for shipyard stays, timber for crates to carry ammunition.

The pall that hung over Gwydyr in 1938 had been ominous enough. The dark clouds of 1939 were lower. Jim Shaw wondered how many of his trained men would go, and how he could keep on planting the trees that the next generation would need as desperately as they were needed now.

9

A Wider Vista

GWYDYR Forest wasn't by any means the only one planted by the Forestry Commission in North Wales. There were others already clothing the mountain slopes and overlooking the winding rivers of the Welsh countryside. In 1939 tree-planters were busy everywhere. When they notified Jim Shaw that he was to become District Officer in charge of five other forests in his area, he was still occupied with the problem of the fire-ravaged part of Gwydyr where the scorched earth showed and black, charred trees still stood pointing grimly at the sky. It might have been enough to work on and make good the loss without looking elsewhere, but Jim Shaw was in the tradition of the old Scots foresters and a determined and dedicated fellow. He inspected his new domain. It covered Cywyd at Corwen on Deeside, Coed y Brenin— the king's wood—at Dolgellau, and Beddgelert, the forest surrounding Gelert's grave, Hafod Fawr, one of the older conifer forests of North Wales at Festiniog, and Clocaenog at Ruthin. All of these were predominantly conifer forests. They were planted with Sitka and Norway spruce, Japanese larch, Douglas fir and Scots pine. As always, timber supply people were searching for trees. They were importuning foresters for thinnings for pitprops and whatever larger trees might be felled for the war. The army was on hand, seeking places in which they might safely train artillerymen in the use of field guns, bombs and the paraphernalia of war.

Jim Shaw looked at Gwydyr in the snow of '39. It seemed a little less scarred when the blackened dead trees were partially clothed in white. It was still a peaceful place and when the snow of that bitterly cold mid-winter melted someone would have to get on with planning and planting. The stark outlines of the plantation blocks were emphasised by the smooth snow rides between. Regarding them from the high parts of the forest Jim Shaw thought they looked like some great factory site, roads and walls and roofs, half-covered with snow. One day, perhaps, the bombers would come and put incendiaries down on those blacked-out 'buildings', and fire would run through it all, going faster and more furiously than it had ever done before. In the meantime he had other things to occupy his mind, how to supply what might be needed for the war effort and keep the forest. Cutting trees down was easy enough. Thinning was always necessary but he would promise only what, as a sound sylviculturist, he knew was in the interests of the long-term development of the woods and it was a blessing that no one could compel him to cut trees indiscriminately.

The fellers, the soldiers and the rest arrived and were absorbed into the different areas along with the forest staff already employed there. More thinnings were barked and stacked on the forest roads. 6,000 tons went out year by year, ten from every acre mature enough to be thinned. The axe and saw, like the guns the soldiers brought, were implements of war. The guns chattered and threw tracer across gorges where there was no danger of fire. Men strained and struggled with bogged-down trucks and carriers, dismantled their field pieces and sent them swinging and swaying, gun, limber and transport wheels, over rocky ravines. The soldiers played at war. The fellers cut the trees that had been planted ten or twenty years before, eight- or nine-inch diameter firs for props and spindly poles, harvested for the furniture trade. The small poles were suddenly important. Utility furniture was the order of the day and the poles were for turnery, becoming legs for chairs and tables that no self-respecting newly-weds would have bought before the war. That the wood was neither mature nor stable hardly mattered. There is a war on, the people said. It was not a catastrophe if a chair keeled over or a table rocked. People were lucky to be alive with a roof over their heads. The blitz was bringing buildings down and burning roofs. It was also burning the very ladders from which the firemen fought the blaze. Some of the long poles needed for firemen's ladders came from Gwydyr. They were fine tall trees that had survived the 1938 fire. Split down, they made thirty-foot rails. Marking his thinning records and classifying the product of his earlier years of labour Jim Shaw took a certain satisfaction from the knowledge that his plans, approved by his superiors at that time, had proved successful. The young forest was producing what it could, even ladders for the blitz. There was anxiety over the submarines Hitler was sending farther and farther out into the Atlantic. In the First World War although the U-boats were out, timber imports had been in no way curtailed. Now importing would cease. Timber might be needed but food and munitions cargoes were more important. The forests of the country as a whole would have to supply what was needed and if there was any significant thing to be marked it was that trees took longer to replace than a regiment of young soldiers.

Forest amenity was not the concern of the nation at war, especially when fine buildings as well as slums were being reduced to rubble. In the planting areas of his six forests Jim Shaw's regiments of fir and larch stood massed in their thousands, covering what had been upland grazings and rocky pastures, waterlogged bogs and peat plateaux. Here and there, however, mindful of future generations,

Jim Shaw saw to it that more attractive and less regimented tree-planting took place along the roadsides. In these places he would have red oak and cherry, a cedar or cypress, and he would spare the slender, handsome silver birch that thrust its way up and stood gracefully in the sun. The soft green leaf of an oak relieves the eye and a birch tree is a thing of beauty.

The labour force in the forests had been augmented by a women's corps, supplemented, when young men left to join up, by men who had opted to do otherwise as conscientious objectors. The forest small-holdings were worked by their tenants, some of them rehabilitated coal miners who had been settled in them in 1929, buying chickens and pigs and milking cows with their government grants. The women foresters were hardly strong enough to perform all the forester's tasks. They cleared land and weeded in the nurseries, eighteen of them at Gwydyr and thirty at Dolgellau. The world was changing everywhere. Women were driving tractors and ploughing and harvesting the land. In the forest, if the women couldn't swing a felling axe there were plenty of other tasks waiting to be done. At night the German planes droned over to bomb Liverpool and Mersey docks. The air-raid siren was heard across the sleeping forests. People became familiar with the sinister, intermittent throb of a German bomber as it headed for some far-off conflagration, or came limping back again across mountains and plantations.

Jim Shaw was in uniform again, the uniform of the Home Guard. He had become accustomed to alarms and alerts but he always sighed with relief at the all-clear. The dread of fire on a large scale never left him. He had an eagle's view of his forests in his mind, especially when the moon was full, and they seemed more than ever like a great complex of factories or warehouses. A bomb, a few incendiaries, would bring light where there had been shadow. The bomb-aimer might tell his captain that he had been mistaken but the forest would be on fire. It didn't happen often, and it never brought the disaster that a fire bomb might have produced had it been dropped on one of those warm, dry nights of high summer. When there was an incident Jim Shaw would inspect the damage, report on it, and assure any forest tenant that he would be supported in his legitimate claims for compensation.

There was a night at Clocaenog, when people stood still and wondered as the ground shook beneath their feet. A German plane, returning with a landmine intended for a Liverpool factory, came low over the forest. Youngsters on the forest road, on their way home after some adventure in the dark, looked up and saw the black outline of the slow-flying bomber. Here was something to have fun with! A stricken bomber that would never get home! They pulled out their torches and flashed lights at the machine. They yelled derisively when it lurched a little, and then they saw the silver ball that was the base of the landmine. The plane was lifting because it had released the burden it had been carrying! It gained height as the youngsters dropped their torches and threw themselves into a ditch. The explosion gusted like a wind round the crags of a mountain. Foliage rippled and grass lay back. The angry red light broadened and became as bright and white as day. Earth and stones and roots fell all round the crater. The dishevelled youngsters rose and tottered home, leaving their torches on the ground. The bomber was by then long gone across the dark Welsh hills. The following day Jim Shaw inspected the scene. He smiled to himself at the escape the youngsters had had. He had known what it was to have a charmed life. It was better that a few yards of forest had been blown up than houses in some densely populated area.

There was only one casualty at Clocaenog Forest, and not a human one at that. At Hendre Farm the old cockerel was a highly-thought-of member of the family. He crowed the dawn for all he was worth. He walked the midden with arrogant pride, raking straw with his over-long spurs and lording it over his harem of scrawny hens. He disdained to perch where lesser fowl perched. After filling his crop and stalking to and fro to pick at the kitchen door, he would take himself to perch in isolation in the piggery. Here, at intervals in the evening he might croon alarm at the passing of the fox, or cluck, once in a while, when he caught a glimpse of an owl flying silently to the ridge of the out-buildings. On this particular night he sat brooding as the German came near, and then he straightened on the perch and raised his head and clucked alarm. The air must have been disturbed by the falling of the landmine, and the churning of the propellers of the machine as it rose again. Perhaps the cockerel heard the explosion and knew his time had come. A whirling fragment of steel burst through the piggery door and struck him in the chest. Whatever indignation he had ended instantly. He fell and his feet made running movements in the straw beneath his perch. His wings flapped and then the blue lids closed over his eyes and he was dead.

'How did Hendre stand up to the explosion?' Jim Shaw asked the old farmer when he made his inspection. 'It shook you, I don't doubt?'

The old man squinted and rubbed his grey, unshaven chin. He scratched himself and announced, 'I will expect compensation from them for this! There was loss, wass there not?'

Jim Shaw looked about for obvious signs of damage. The stone walls of Hendre were intact. The explosion had been fifty yards or more from the buildings, and on the blind side where there was no glass.

'The door of the pigsty, maybe?' he suggested, seeing the shattered wood.

'The door of my pigsty, of course,' said the farmer, 'but also the death of my cockerel. He wass a fine bird. They should pay for him, I think so.'

It was hard to deny the old fellow. The piggery door

would have to be made good, even if there was no pig in the sty. The death of an old, long-spurred cockerel whose stiff body lay on the straw barely amounted to a serious claim for war damage.

'If you put in a claim I will support you,' he said. 'Damage to the door, and the loss of one cockerel!'

'A very special cockerel,' insisted the old man. 'Like one of the family he wass.'

Jim Shaw was compelled to agree. The evidence was there. The cockerel had died from shrapnel in the chest. He would never again crow the coming of day over Clocaenog.

'You must put him down on your claim then,' he said, wondering what the civil service would make of it. He could imagine a claims officer marking it 'not granted' and adding a footnote that the cockerel had probably gone into the cooking pot.

'We can't very well eat him,' said the old man, as though reading his mind. 'Too old and too tough he wass.'

There was more excitement when a 'German' was found hanging in one of the trees of Gwydyr, however. One of Jim Shaw's men, convinced that something out of the ordinary had happened within his territory, made search of the forest around Betws-y-Coed. A man had baled out from a plane. He was quite sure of that, and he knew the locality in which the parachutist had dropped. Quite alone, the forester Home Guard tackled the invader when he found him dangling from the tree.

'Come down out of there!' he ordered. 'Come down, and keep your hands above your head!'

It was easy enough to keep his hands above his head, but the airman found it difficult to get to the ground until he was helped and prodded with the rifle. He disentangled himself from the remains of his parachute harness and did his best to march when he was ordered to march. Over his shoulder he gave his name, rank and number. The name

was decidedly German, it seemed to his captor, Macksimchunk.

'Keep marching, and don't take your hands off your
head!'

They marched in the darkness all the way down to
Betws-y-Coed.

'Nationality?' asked Jim Shaw.

'German!' said the man who had brought the prisoner.

'Canadian,' said the prisoner. 'Name, Macksimchunk'

'Very likely,' agreed Jim Shaw. 'Since you can't prove
any of that, and I've nowhere to hold you, we'll take you
down to the police station.

Jim had loaded his Browning automatic. The prisoner
was bundled into his car and kept covered while they
trundled along to the police. Macksimchunk was pale and
trembling. His condition didn't improve when the police
sergeant decided he was a spy to be locked up at once. Jim
Shaw would have none of that. If the prisoner's identity
couldn't be confirmed he must still be handed over to the
military. This was in accordance with regulations, whatever side their captive proved to belong to,

'Take him away then,' said the sergeant. 'You'll save
me making book entries and reports. If I were you I'd
shoot him!'

Macksimchunk groaned as Jim Shaw hustled him out
and took him off to the army.

'Macksimchunk?' said the army. 'It sounds outlandish.
Canadian? Well, maybe. On the other hand he might be
an impostor. We'll sort him out.'

Jim Shaw went home to bed. In the morning the
telephone rang. Macksimchunk was Macksimchunk,
Canadian Air Force sergeant, and not a spy or German
parachutist. There had been a suggestion that before
he baled out again he should change his name to something more British.

When the men of the mountain artillery came to the
forest they brought their mules with them. The mules

cropped grass and behaved in the manner of their kind, flicking their ears and showing the whites of their eyes as they lashed out with their small hooves in moments of stress. The artillerymen levered their limbers out of pot-holes, cursed a lot and fell out to smoke on command. It worried Jim Shaw that the men were not allowed to smoke except at fixed times. He knew the way of soldiers and could imagine them cupping stumps of cigarettes in their palms and dropping them when there was danger of being discovered. The surreptitious smoker might set the forest on fire. It was a great relief to him when the artillerymen left to use their mules and guns in other places and the forests were left in peace again.

In Betws-y-Coed there were many evacuees from Liverpool and London. Boys of Dulwich College had been sent there for safety and their headmaster approached Jim Shaw to see if some of his older pupils might contribute to the war effort by working in the forest. The offer was accepted and the boys were soon armed with saws and pruning tools and instructed how to use them. They worked well and enjoyed an outdoor existence. Before they went back to Dulwich Jim Shaw had them plant their own section of young trees to mark their stay in North Wales.

The war in Europe ended, and finally Japan surrendered. The forests stood green and healthy, little the worse for all that had happened in six years. What could a man ask for more than to see his labour bearing fruit but the Commission had other plans for Jim Shaw now. Was he not a man with almost unique experience of private estate and woodland management? He was invited to move to Shrewsbury to become responsible for private woodlands, advising estate owners on how they might replant and restore woods that had suffered during the war. Eight counties of Wales would come under his jurisdiction. While state forests—those under the Commission—had recourse to government funds and treasury loans, private

woodland owners were in a different situation. A wood is
easily felled and its timber hurried to the mill, but afterwards money is needed for clearing and replanting. Few
owners had money or labour to cope with the problem.
The woodlands Dedication Scheme had been instigated
to meet the need for state support. Under it, a grant of
75 per cent could be made to an owner undertaking to
restore his own woodland. The most important stipulation
under this scheme was that restored woodland must be
dedicated in perpetuity to timber production. Mature
trees, once at their prime, must be cut to provide timber
for the market. This, in the case of conifer or hardwood
trees, would be in the national interest and justify the
grant.

There were more than 9,000 acres of private woodlands
in the eight counties of Anglesey, Caernarvon, Denbigh,
Flint, Merioneth, Carmarthen, Radnor, and Cardigan at
this time, part of it deciduous, although in the main conifer
woods. Jim Shaw's task was to survey woods and advise
their owners on the restoration of devastated areas. He also
had to explain to them the ways in which they might obtain
assistance. An acre of trees could be efficiently planted for
as little as £25, but the money had to be spent before a
grant was made. Manpower was scarce. It was needed
everywhere for a variety of purposes. A great many men
were still in the Services, some of them owners of the very
woods Jim Shaw had to survey. There was the old, inbuilt
distrust of the busybody civil servant to be overcome. No
one welcomes an official who seems to intrude in a private
domain.

Jim Shaw, checking his maps and files at Shrewsbury,
knew it wouldn't be easy. He remembered how jealous
his father had been of their rights and privileges at Killearn
estate. It had been a very private world, a kingdom of its
own. No one had dared give advice on how it should be
run without being invited to do so. A man with less tact
than Jim Shaw might have come to grief in a short time,

but Shaw knew private estates as few others in the Commission knew them. He had lived within that hierarchy. He knew the outlook of agents, factors, farm managers, bailiffs and others employed in the private sphere. It bothered him a little that many of the woodland owners were still away and many hadn't walked through their own woods in six years or more, being serving soldiers. He sat down and wrote to the 'absentee' landlords, informing them of his intention of calling upon their agents or bailiffs to discuss the problem of reafforestation and the dedication scheme. He followed up and called upon the occupier or tenant. Tactfully he would suggest that they might discuss the problem as they walked through what was left of the woods.

'A tree takes forty to sixty years to grow into something you may profitably sell, often longer,' he would say. 'I am not suggesting that what I am instructed to put to you is something you must do this year or next. It is in your interest and the interest of the country that your woodlands be re-established. It is my job to help you do that.'

Almost invariably he was well received. After all, few people who owned woods and knew anything at all about them could resist a man who so obviously loved trees and was concerned to see them growing. Jim Shaw walked with an owner and moved the brushwood or bracken to reveal naturally seeded trees, stool shoots rising where old trees had been felled.

'There,' he would say with great enthusiasm, 'your wood is growing again! All it needs is some encouragement. You can't ask for more than a naturally seeded tree. What has to be done is the debris taken away, the undergrowth cut back and the trees allowed to regenerate. You'll have to plant a few hundred seedlings, but I can get these for you when you are ready!'

They would begin to plot and count the seedlings, conjuring up a picture of a young wood growing as they went on from place to place. In any given area of brush-wood and scrub there will be a certain number of trees naturally seeded. A forester knows how to make a wood and how to encourage its regeneration.

What grows naturally on the land is always hard to dis-courage and when trees are cut down it is only the trunk or pole that is wanted. The remainder, the twigs, the branches and the stump remain where the axemen leave them littering the floor of the wood. In a month or two ferns, foxglove and ragged robin, bracken and bramble all begin to rise because they have seeded, being shaded and supplied with more moisture than before. In half a year creeping elder, ivy and a dozen other wild plants compete and the strongest and most prolific weave themselves into a tangle that the old dead branches support. Soon the place that was once a wood is an almost impenetrable jungle. The wilderness consolidates itself more and more in a wet summer when the briars and brambles thicken. It is a daunting sight to a man who has never had to tackle the business of clearing land and planting it. Pioneers in Canada carved their homes from the forests with the same desperation that a novice tackles this kind of thing. Jim Shaw knew how depressing the scene was to men who came back to find that the fellers had never burned a branch nor bothered whether unwanted trees blocked any future access to the place. He would explain how the work might be done, the brambles and briars slashed and trailed off to be piled and fired along with the remains of the felled trees. In every case the backbreak and blisters would come when the ground was reclaimed. Planting would be simple enough and a great relief from all that had gone before. Woods, like fields of wheat, were cultivated. Jungles were a natural product of the wild, uncultivated land, breeding disease, seeding weeds, closing off what man had toiled for generations to hold as his own.

'All very well, Mr Shaw,' some small woodland owner would say, agreeing that what had been his he must recover, 'but how can I find the men to clear up the mess when I have only one old gardener and two farm labourers on my staff?'

Who had brought the wood to such a state? The fellers, the contractors who had come to haul away the timber. They had bought the timber. Perhaps now they could be persuaded to hire themselves out to clear the ground once again, clear it of the fallen trees, the elders, the rank growth their haste and untidiness had brought about. Jim Shaw went off to talk to the contractors. They weren't quite so busy as they had been when the war was on and almost anything was justified on the ground of expediency. Timber was being imported and there were fewer trees to be cut down. Many of them were glad of the opportunity of employing their men on clearing and planting. There were drawbacks to this, of course for the contractors had to transport their men every day and there was a danger that some of them would spend longer travelling and brewing tea over their fires than they did clearing and planting. Progress of any kind was better than none at all, however. Finding men or finding money, Jim Shaw did what he could.

That some of the still absent soldiers had financial problems when it came to investing in the tree-planting business was made plain from the correspondence Jim Shaw had with them or their agents.

'There are urgent things like the repair of buildings and the replacement of worn-out implements that have first call on what money the estate had,' an agent would tell him. 'We just haven't the cash to provide £2,500 to plant 100 acres of trees, even if we are to get it back.'

What had estates like Killearn done when money was needed to maintain gates, barns etc? They always asked the forester to mark trees for felling. It was true that in some of these small Welsh estates the demand for timber had left them bare of trees, but never quite so bare that a few trees did not remain. A survey of what trees there were and an assessment of their value on the market often showed that the money could be raised. Jim Shaw would see to it that the merchant gave the best price for this bottom-of-the-barrel scraping of trees. The money was spent on clearing and planting and the grant claimed as soon as possible to allow even more clearing and planting to be undertaken.

Correspondence with the absentee soldier gave him great satisfaction when he was able to tell him that things were going well.

'You probably remember the wood the way it was when you were shooting there before the outbreak of war. It isn't the place you remember, of course, but we have started to make good the damage. You will be glad that it was done and your wood will rise again if not in your time at least in your children's time. If there is any way I can help you now or at any future time you must let me know. I have impressed upon your people here that I view my role as that of your private forester rather than a civil servant. The urgency of re-afforestating may be over-stressed to a certain degree. It really doesn't matter if things can't be done this year or even next year so long as we get them done. A year is nothing when a tree takes a lifetime to grow. All that matters is that every acre that can be cleared and replanted is replanted in the end. The Commission have their own programme of planting on land acquired for that purpose but it would be futile if the private woods were allowed to deteriorate and ceased to exist. I am sure you will see how important this is. . . .'

The work involved Jim Shaw in a great deal of travelling about the country. He went down into Radnor, into Carmarthenshire. He inspected woods that had made their contribution to the war effort and looked as depressing in some cases as the derelict pillboxes and gunsites along the coast of Wales. If there had been secret and secluded woods before the war during it they had been discovered. Woods where kites had sailed and buzzards nested had been invaded and the heart cut out of them. His task was to see that trees were planted. He lived hopefully and was happy to think that he was making a contribution to the recovery of the woods and the country's ultimate wealth.

There were still places where trees were being taken. Timber was needed for the building trade. Contractors persuaded owners of woods to apply for felling orders. When a felling order was requested Jim Shaw would be asked to give his verdict on the state of the timber to be cut or left growing. He had to assess the quality and quantity of timber a section of woodland would yield, taking care to see that the order was filled without the merchants getting more than their due. He had been taught to assess the cubic capacity of timber in a given area by his father, and men like Davy Carr, so that he could walk through a wood and estimate with confidence. It amused him to see how impressed some of the merchants were when he did this. His father had loved to do the same thing, adding a few cubic feet to his round figure estimate and slyly watching their faces as they made a note of the timber to be felled. Felling was as much a part of the forester's business as planting but Shaw was glad that the days of widespread felling and ruthless extraction of timber had come to an end. Now he was devoting himself to planting rather than cutting down. Even when he gave his verdict on a felling order he found himself thinking of the clearing and planting that would shortly begin. A time for planting? There was no particular time. It must go on continually, year in and year out. What had Davy Carr told him? Aye be putting in a tree. . . .

10

Retirement

EDITH SHAW died in 1953, just three years before Jim was due to retire. They had moved to Shrewsbury in 1946, not because they had in any way hankered for town life, but because Jim Shaw had climbed another rung of the ladder. The thought of retirement hadn't burdened them at all when what they looked forward to was to live in a house in the shelter of a wood and look out on trees, to cultivate a garden, gather sticks for the fire. Jim Shaw had seen himself doing these things, as his father had done them, even if retirement on a private estate in his father's day had been almost unheard of while a man had his health and strength. Shrewsbury was a pleasant enough town. From its more elevated parts a man could look at the wooded countryside of Shropshire and far off places that had inspired Mary Webb, but it was a dreary town and a dreary world in 1953. Bereaved, Jim Shaw had little to stay his frequent bouts of misery but his work. He was still involved in the problems of the Dedication of Woodlands Scheme. People continued to write to the Commission about their difficulties, and their doubts that anyone could receive money for planting trees on their own land. Some of the problems needed more than a little thought and Jim Shaw frequently found himself drawing upon the experience of his apprentice days and the advice he had been given then. Perhaps some of the enquiries he received might have had less detailed attention had he not found that it was better to work at his desk than to go home where everything reminded him of his wife. He took pride in being able to plan the recovery of land that had gone back to the wild and in the opportunity to make woodlands from what had been scrub and wilderness. Whatever the form-filling and clerical work might involve, the end was forestry and the planting of trees.

There were, of course, other matters to occupy his time. He was recruited to help with the Royal Welsh Show and became a director of the show committee. At the annual show he met old friends and people who had sought his advice, writing to him from the farthermost corners of the principality. Trees and woodlands may be close to a man's door, but few people know enough about them to cultivate them or cut them down without expert advice. The Royal Welsh Show embraced forestry and the skills required of woodmen. The sort of people Jim Shaw needed to have contact with sought him out once a year to have what they hoped to do or planned to do confirmed. He was almost as fond of this kind of man as he was of trees. When someone told him of the progress of a wood he had helped to establish he was delighted. He could talk endlessly about thinning and the way of felling ripe timber so that the remaining trees would continue to thrive. He had seen the mistakes of the early days of conifer planting on a large scale and the benefit of that experience was what most of his contacts sought.

That he had done his job well Jim Shaw never paused to think. He was a man who had always plodded on, eager to tackle the thing that lay before him. In 1956, the year of his retirement, he reached a point, when, in spite of himself he found himself thinking about what he had done, and how others regarded his efforts. He hadn't expected official recognition, but there it was, a summons to London to receive the M.B.E. 'I have the honour to inform you that

The Queen will hold an Investiture at Buckingham Palace on Tuesday November 13th 1956, at which your attendance is requested,' the communication ran. He read it and read it again. He thought about his father and the Killearn estate. A man did what he chose to do and earned his living doing it. He did not need to love his work but accepted that he had to do it. In his own case, and like his father, he had loved his work. Now for some reason he was considered to have contributed more than he needed to have done. At least what he had done was appreciated. There was a degree of satisfaction in that, although sadness overtook him when he thought how he would have enjoyed handing the letter to Edith and asking her what she would wear to go to the Palace. The sun will shine on you one day, Davy Carr had told him. Old men often encouraged youth with words of this kind, but now the recollection held significance. Davy had been looking down at him while he worked on his knees in the nursery, clearing weeds that were choking the seedling trees with hands that were both chapped and blue. If the words had warmed his heart a little his hands hadn't become less numb!

There wasn't much sun in the November sky on the way from Shrewsbury to London. A grey haze hung above the city that morning. He remembered living in London. He remembered seeing it for the first time as a young soldier on his way to the guards depot. It looked as grim as ever. He straightened his back and walked upright through the Palace gateway out of respect for the guardsmen who stamped and pounded their measured distance, smiling a little at the thought of those seemingly endless hours under the command of the drill sergeants. The steps he ascended reminded him of a time when he went to the big house carrying his father's newly-caught salmon to his master. There were others there awaiting the summons. He nodded and smiled and wondered about them until his name was called. He received his decoration thinking of old Davy Carr again. The old Highlandman

must have had second sight because a ray of sunshine from
a high window made him screw up his eyes and blink.
There was no way of finding out for Davy Carr and his
father were long gone to tend the woods on the far side of
the Styx.

The end of the road with the Forestry Commission and
the M.B.E. would have been more welcome had Jim
Shaw been able to retire with his wife as his companion in
his less active years. He was not an old man. Contrary to
what some people are inclined to think long days out of
doors, planting trees in driving rain and extremes of cold
had not brought on rheumatism or impaired his ability to
do what he had to do. He could still keep his end up on a
crosscut saw when he chose to do so. He could still fell a
tree with a few clean, precise strokes with a felling axe.
He could, if necessary, clear ground and plant to demonstrate the right way of doing the thing, and he loved both
the practical and technical side of his work as much as
ever. The only irksome thing about his latter days had
been a predominance of paper-work and his over-occupa-
tion with clerical matters which seems invariably to go
with a more responsible position. Now, perhaps, he would
be able to get back to his proper element, the living wood,
and find free-lance work as an adviser.

There were a great many people who needed to know
the way of going about things when it came to applying
for grants for replanting projects. Contractors, too, had
already come knocking at his door. He was, after all, well-
versed in the intracacies of timber control. He knew
about felling orders and preservation orders. He had the
eye of an assessor and knew when timber would ripen and
whether its value would appreciate by delaying the
decision to cut it down. He could deal with hardwood and
softwood problems and loved the variety of work that had
involved a lifetime's experience.

One of the estate owners who approached him as his
days with the Commission were nearing their end was a

member of the Gladstone family, owners of Hawarden
Castle and Hawarden Estate in Flintshire. Hawarden's
woodlands, like those of many another estate that had
suffered the ravages of war and years of compulsory
neglect, were in need of immediate attention. For a
considerable time the estate had been without the services
of a trained forester. They had had a woodman, but there
is a great difference between a mere axeman and a forester,
between a clearer of paths and a man versed in sylviculture
A woodman doesn't need to know how to encourage
growth or give light and air to a part of a wood that can
become a natural seedbed. He very often doesn't bother to
check the obvious signs of disease or curb the spread of a
parasite which may reduce a wood to derelict scrubland.
The Hawarden agent was well aware of the need for
professional attention to something that was, after all, an
important asset, something to be improved by re-invest-
ment. Although Jim Shaw had no particular wish to go
back to his beginnings and become an estate forester, here
was an opportunity to work once again in private forestry
with the full authority of an estate forester, which was
what the Gladstone estate offered. His father's freedom
had been unexceptional in its day but his father had worked
in a country where forestry on the private estate lacking
many of the resources of the more lavishly endowed
southern properties was understood and rated of prime
importance. Now, with a more enlightened outlook, most
estates were inclined to take stock of potential assets and
take advantage of what encouragement the government
was giving. It didn't take Jim Shaw long to make up his
mind. He accepted the Hawarden offer and became a part-
time estate forester. The work would fit in well enough
with his arrangement to make his home with his son who,
after service in the Army, was in charge of a forest in
mid-Wales. In a short time Jim Shaw was walking the
Hawarden woods, making up his mind what would have
to be done to restore them. Some of these woods were in

danger of becoming derelict. He listed them as he walked, Bilberry Wood and High Park Wood, Price's Hill, Silverwell, Young Squire's, Tinker's Dale and Mill Wood taking note of the rough acreage of sycamore and elm. A good part of Hawarden's trees were broad-leaved.

No task in forestry is likely to show either a quick result or a rapid return. The Hawarden woods had at least fifty acres in need of clearing and replanting. Labour was almost as scarce as it had been ten years earlier. There had always been a drift away from the land and the hardships of outdoor work. Not many youngsters saw their future in forestry. Jim Shaw got on with the task of restoring the woods but he was concerned to ultimately have more leisure and enjoy his retirement more fully. He found a pupil close at hand in young Frank Mills, whose family gave their blessing to his study of forestry. Jim Shaw didn't consciously think back to his own apprenticeship and the help he had had from Davy Carr, but he did all he could to instil into his protégé the things old Davy had taught him about woodland management. He set Frank Mills questions to which he required answers in writing, urged him to attend lectures at the nearby estate of the Duke of Westminster, and generally behaved towards him like a schoolmaster. Frank Mills was an apt and willing pupil. He sat and passed his Woodman's Certificate. Soon afterwards he took the Royal English Forestry Society's Forester's Certificate and finally obtained his National Diploma in Forestry. This was no small achievement for either pupil or master.

Hawarden woods had certainly shown visible signs of care and attention. Jim Shaw was delighted when, in the open competition at the Royal Welsh Show, the estate won first prize for the quality and condition of its firwood, first for its hurdles and gates made from larch poles, and its woodmen a prize for cleaving oak stakes. Young Frank Mills was duly confirmed in the position of Estate Forester at Hawarden when Jim Shaw left to retire completely. It was natural that when he did retire he should find a home in the forest of Gwydyr, which he had known and cultivated almost from its infancy. Donald Shaw had become Warden of Gwydyr and the family moved back to Betws-y-Coed.